CONCURRENT PC DOS

CONCURRENT PC DOS

PHIL BALMA
JOE BYRD
JOE GUZAITIS
JIM NEEDHAM
KEVIN WANDRYK

PRENTICE-HALL
Englewood Cliffs, New Jersey 07632

Library of Congress Cataloging-in-Publication Data
Main entry under title:

Concurrent PC DOS.

Includes index.
1. Concurrent PC DOS (Computer operating system)
I. Balma, Phil.
QA76.76.O63C66   1986   005.4'46   85-30167
ISBN 0-13-167271-1

Editorial/production supervision and
   interior design: Nancy Menges/David Ershun
Cover design: Photo Plus Art
Manufacturing buyer: Gordon Osbourne
Cover photo Courtesy of Tom G. O'Neal, Admakers

LIMITS OF LIABILITY AND DISCLAIMER OF WARRANTY:

The author and publisher of this book have used their best efforts in preparing this
book. These efforts include the development, research, and testing of
the theories and programs to determine their effectiveness. The author and
publisher make no warranty of any kind, expressed or implied, with regard to these
programs or the documentation contained in this book. The author and publisher
shall not be liable in any event for incidental or consequential damages in
connection with, or arising out of, the furnishing, performance, or use
of these programs.

Printed in the United States of America

10 9 8 7 6 5 4 3 2 1

ISBN 0-13-167271-1   025

CONTENTS

FOREWORD

I want to explain where we came from and why we got to where we are in concurrency and multitasking, and to provide a little bit of historical perspective. Sometimes it's frustrating to see a new technology that is not widely accepted by society. This certainly occurred for us at Digital Research with multitasking, which we saw as an important concept in small-computer uses.

Our company, in fact, has always been commercially oriented. At first, MP/M was an 8-bit multitasking operating system that had support for networking through CPNet. We had mixed reviews on MP/M-80, basically because people said that microcomputers couldn't easily support multitasking because of their limited memory size.

As an example, the success of MP/M on Altos computer systems stemmed from their support of bankswitched memory. Bankswitched memory allowed an 8-bit processor to access a lot more than just 64K. In fact, Altos systems at that time could access 208K of memory, which represents a fairly large 16-bit machine right now, through their own bankswitched memory systems.

Sixteen-bit systems were a godsend for people working on operating systems at Digital Research. An 8088- or 8086-based system was really just an 8-bit microprocessor-based system with built-in bankswitched memory. The speed of the processor was fundamentally the same, not much faster; and certainly the instruction set was basically the same.

When 16-bit machines came into the marketplace, we used multitasking as our primary focus to make the transition from the 8-bit to the 16-bit world. We changed the name from MP/M to Concurrent CP/M, and we put more work into the real-time nucleus of the operating system and the multiaccess file system. We believed the world was moving toward multitasking as a fundamental concept for small computers. Following the lead we had started in multitasking and concurrency, we knew that networking was also required for a commercial operating environment and that networking is difficult without multitasking.

One drawback of the emerging 16-bit machines was that they were built on the Apple II model—that is, small disk systems with basically small memory systems. They were not capable of taking advantage of concurrent systems.

These days, with the introduction of larger memory systems and faster processors, personal computers can rival the power and capabilities of low-end minicomputer systems. These more capable personal computers demand commercial languages, multitasking, concurrency, networking, and data communications. It's gratifying to see that the marketplace now sees multitasking as an absolute requirement for the future evolution of small computers. We didn't believe that single-tasking systems would last long, but they have been popular for a couple of years now. As a result, the CP/M-86 was really a bridge into the concurrent multitasking world.

Now, with Concurrent PC DOS, we have an operating system that provides not only multitasking but also multiuser capabilities to the 16-bit computer. When we developed Concurrent, we felt it was necessary to make it available to as many existing applications as possible. Therefore, we have designed it to run both CP/M and DOS applications at the same time. Concurrent PC DOS also makes available the widest range of commercial languages, networking, and data communications features offered today. With Concurrent PC DOS, microcomputers can begin to achieve their full potential and truly to rival the low-end minicomputer systems.

Dr. Gary Kildall

INTRODUCTION TO A CONCURRENT
PROCESSING ENVIRONMENT

Concurrent is the term used to describe the operating systems from Digital Research that have revolutionized the working environment of the micro-computer. Simply put, Concurrent allows a microcomputer to act like several computers, doing different jobs simultaneously while you interact with each job only as you need to.

To understand how and why Concurrent was created, we need to explore the environment in which it was developed. In this chapter we see how impatience with the single-tasking working environment created the impetus to bring multitasking from the world of the mainframe to that of the microcomputer.

IMPATIENCE IS THE MOTHER OF CONCURRENT

As the microcomputer gains broader acceptance and wider use in business, there is an inclination to have it take over more and more of the tedious or complex tasks that daily confront the "knowledge worker." Coupled with this is the need to get maximum use out of these systems because they represent such a large investment to an organization.

These are the two questions that are most often asked: (1) How do we make the worker more efficient? (2) How do we get more work out of the machine? One answer to the first question is to gather the tools around the worker so that less time is spent going somewhere to get a tool that is needed to do a job.

This is essentially what you are doing when you have to exit one program to load another—running back and forth from the "tool crib" to check out and then return "tools." You are exiting your word processor and then loading your spreadsheet; exiting your spreadsheet and getting into a data base. Then you load the word processor again to put all the information together. Until now that was the way it had to be done. Some serious workers have several computers gathered around them in order to save time while they do extended processing with long-running routines such as sorting or searching. This method is effective but expensive.

THE OFFICE ENVIRONMENT

Looking at this process in the office environment makes the point even more clearly. Consider the following scenario. You have in front of you:

1. A notepad
2. A calculator
3. A business card file
4. A telephone

These are your main tools, although you also rely on the contents of your filing cabinet, reference books, dictionary, and typewriter. What if you had to get up from your chair, go across the room, unlock the filing cabinet, take out one of these items, and then go back to your desk to use it?

For example, you use the notepad to draft a report. When you stop writing on the notepad, you put it into in the cabinet and then remove the calculator and take it back to your desk. When you are through calculating and need to look up the name and address of a customer to include in the report, that's right, back to the cabinet, put back the calculator, take out the card file, back to the desk, look up the name, back to the cabinet, get out the notepad, continue writing the report, and so on. Now that's a ludicrous way to work, isn't it? But most workers who actively use a microcomputer in their work do something similar all day long.

Consider that I load my spreadsheet and begin calculating the bid prices for the report I am writing. When I complete my work, I have to save my calculations and print a copy so that I can refer to them. Then I load my customer name and address file, search for the correct entry, print that entry, unload that file, load my word processor, open a document file, and start typing. Whew! With concurrent processing, on the other hand, you take all your tools and put them in front of you at once and move between them at will. Unlike the worker above, you never have to leave your "chair" for those constant trips to the "tool crib."

Now, let's take this a step further. Besides using each of these tools conveniently one at a time, we can use them in an "overlapping" manner which allows us to do several processes simultaneously. For instance, we could start a complex calculation going on the calculator and let it continue while we start typing a letter on the typewriter or make a phone call. Now we begin to use the full potential of concurrency. On the computer you can have up to four processes running concurrently in this manner.

Here's an example. We can designate each area that we work with a separate window. Therefore, on window 1, we can have a word-processing program doing a lengthy word-replacement function, while on window 2 we have a spelling checker processing a report, and on window 3 we have a spreadsheet doing a lengthy recalculation. At the same time we have been logged on to a remote database with our modem on window 4 looking for some specialized information. This is not wishful thinking; the capability is here today with the Concurrent PC DOS operating system.

THE FOUR LEVELS OF WORK EFFICIENCY

Besides making one person's work environment more productive, groups of workers can be similarly affected. If you can group tools among many workers so that they are convenient (as well as cost-effective by their being shared), so much the better. Let's explore some of the implications of these concepts. Essentially, we are matching workers and tasks.

1. One worker   One task
2. One worker   Many tasks
3. Many workers   One task
4. Many workers   Many tasks

Right now most people using a microcomputer are at the first level. They work on one thing at a time. When they are through with one task, they start another. If the computer becomes tied up sorting data or printing a report, they wait. What if you had to stop the car whenever you wanted to play the radio or a tape. That's the kind of thing that most microcomputers make you do. If you want to print a letter, for instance, you can't do anything else.

At the second level, as we have seen, one worker works on several things "at once," for instance, doing complex calculations while writing a report and also plotting a graph that will be included in the report. This is a case where the Concurrent operating system enables a worker to multiply his or her effort greatly. By allowing the computer to run several programs side by side, as it were, and having the worker switch between them when the need arises, Concurrent processing makes possible higher levels of productivity. Now you can play the radio, turn on the heater, and adjust the mirrors while you are driving down the road.

With many workers sharing a single computer, the third level, there is great economic benefit because the machine will be idle less often. This means that programs can be shared and that software and data do not have to be duplicated. If these workers are working on a common project, there are obvious benefits to their sharing a data base as well as other software tools. For example, several insurance agents could access the same pool of customer information to load into an actuarial program, calculate rates, and then use a word processor to write a letter to a prospective customer—all with speed and convenience never before possible on a microcomputer.

The ultimate computer configuration that maximizes worker efficiency and machine use is represented by the fourth level. By connecting several Concurrent microcomputers together, the benefits of multitasking are combined with the economies of shared resources. This has been a goal of microcomputer users everywhere. Now with Concurrent it is a reality.

We have examined several examples of how concurrency can have a dramatic effect on the "throughput" of a knowledge worker's daily activities. This was extended into group settings, demonstrating how efficiencies can be compounded when many workers share hardware and software as well as the products of their labors. Discussions of concurrency on the microcomputer often have a futuristic ring to them. One expects that these things will be possible tomorrow, but not today. That's not the case. The hardware exists. The software exists. All that is required is implementation.

In the chapters that follow, we will discuss in detail how the power of concurrency, in particular an operating system known as Concurrent PC DOS, can help workers become more productive. We will examine the structure and evolution of this powerful multitasking, multiuser operating system with its diverse complement of utilities and see how it can be incorporated into a variety of work environments.

2

THE DUAL OPERATING-SYSTEM ENVIRONMENT

Concurrent PC DOS evolved from Concurrent CP/M, which in turn evolved from CP/M, the predominant operating system in the 8-bit microcomputer environment. However, PC-DOS and MS-DOS came to be the dominant operating systems in the 16-bit environment. Digital Research has provided an operating system called Concurrent PC-DOS that is not only multitasking and multiuser but also accepts programs written to run under either CP/M-86 or PC-DOS and MS-DOS.

This accommodation is not yet total, however. Most CP/M-86 programs can run, but only certain DOS programs that are "well behaved" (i.e., don't bypass the operating system) can run. Obviously, if a program ignores the restrictions of an operating system and deals directly with the hardware, it can cause havoc. Imagine a reckless driver careening around town ignoring stop signs, red lights, and crosswalks. Disaster is sure to result. Those signs and signals represent the town's "operating system" for the traffic that passes through it. Without such a regulatory system, we get collision, gridlock, and in a word, pandemonium.

Why would anyone want to write a program that goes around the operating system? Well, as in our town traffic example, it is sometimes effective to take a shortcut. It's easier and it saves time. In certain circumstances it works, but shortcuts developed for one operating system usually don't work under another.

Imagine trying to take the same shortcut in a different town. Let's say that your favorite shortcut was the alley behind Front Street in Monterey. It saved you from having to go around the block with a series of one-way streets. But here you are in Carmel and you go to what appears to be the same part of town and Front Street has become Main Street and the alley is a dead end. Your shortcut no longer works.

There are many "well-behaved" DOS application programs, which is why Concurrent PC-DOS is such a powerful operating system. The list of such programs is growing daily as more and more software application developers take advantage of concurrency. See the supplement "Running Applications Under Concurrent PC-POS" to the Digital Research "Operating System User's Guide" for further information (and Appendix E).

The most common situation in terms of dual-operating-system use is when someone has been using one operating system and has invested in a number of application programs for it and then decides to switch to another operating system. Typically, this means that the prior investment is lost.

Let's say that you were running a word processor, a spreadsheet, a filing program, and a graphing program under CP/M-86 on your IBM PC. Over time, you notice that many more programs are available under PC-DOS. However, you have already invested several thousand dollars in software. You are rather fond of some of these programs and do not want to give them up. If you switch to PC-DOS, you have to replace these programs and learn a new operating system before you can take advantage of some of the newer, more powerful programs available. Let's call this the "upgrade" scenario.

The next situation is the reverse. You have an IBM PC or clone, and you have been using PC DOS and have accumulated a software library. But you have noticed that there are certain graphics programs, say, or languages under CP/M-86 that you would very much like to have. Again, you must learn a new operating system and switch environments from one set of applications to another. This is the "branching out" into a new operating system scenario.

Finally, there is the situation where you have already invested in both CP/M-86 and PC-DOS because you felt the needs expressed above, but you are frustrated by the fact that you have to switch command structures as you switch operating system environments. You have also wished that you could have several computers side by side so that you could use several programs at any given time. You might also want to share data between programs running under the two different environments. Let's call this the "wishful thinking" scenario.

There are some people who can juggle the CP/M and PC-DOS environments and run programs under both. They are not in the majority. Most users find it a significant step to switch operating systems, and there had better be a good reason to do so. Many users have felt the need for multitasking on their microcomputer but didn't really expect to see it for quite some time. The combination of multitasking and the ability to run CP/M and DOS programs side by side provides an answer to all these needs.

Let's say that you've invested in Concurrent PC-DOS, brought it home, and installed it on your computer. What do you find? The first pleasant surprise is that many commands are names with which you are familiar. Also, there are programs included that will help with your work. A CARDFILE data base manager is there. A communications program, DR TALK, is also there, together with a printer manager program, a sophisticated menu program, and a window manager program. There's plenty of room to grow as you explore these possibilities. Right now, however, you simply want to see if you can run both types of programs on the same computer at the same time.

When you check the documentation, you find that you are able to run the approved DOS programs. By experimenting you find that all the CP/M-86 programs run well. So for the "upgrade" and "branching" scenarios, you are home free. You can now run programs from both the CP/M and DOS environments.

In the "wishful thinking" scenario, you can run them side by side almost as if you had four computers on the desk in front of you. As you look at the screen you see a status line at the bottom that has three text areas and a white rectangle. (See Figure 2.1) Hold down the Ctrl (control) key and press 1, 2, 3, and 4 on the keypad (not the number keys at the top of the keyboard), and then back to 1 again. Watch as the white rectangle moves down the status line. Each time it moves, the screen flickers and a "new computer" becomes available to you.

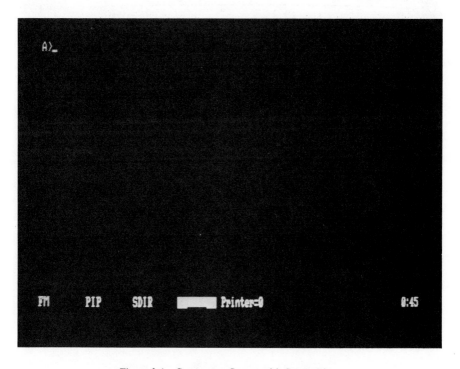

Figure 2.1   Concurrent Screen with Status Line

Put yourself into window 1 (type Ctrl-1). Get a directory listing of your current disk drive by typing in DIR. Press Ctrl-2. Type in 8087. (This shows whether the 8087 coprocessor is on or off.) This is just something different to put on the screen. Now press Ctrl-3 and type in the word PRINTER. (This shows the number of the printer that is assigned to that window.) Now press Ctrl-4 and type in STOP. (This shows all the programs that are running and allows you to stop them.)

You now have something in each window. You have been given built-in commands so that it didn't matter which disks you had loaded. These commands and others are part of the operating system. Now, for a bit of fun, press Ctrl-1, 2, 3, and 4 in rapid succession and see what happens. That is, hold down Ctrl and press 1, 2, 3, and 4 on the keypad rapidly.

Each command you entered has generated a display on a different window (Figure 2.2). In similar fashion you can load different programs doing different work built to run under different operating systems in different windows and have them run side by side on the same computer. That is the true accomplishment of Concurrent PC-DOS.

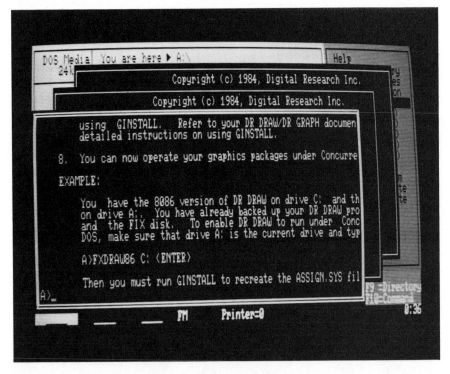

Figure 2.2 Four Concurrent Screens

THE FINE PRINT

There are some limitations on the types of programs that can be run in the manner described above. Most CP/M programs and languages will run without trouble since Concurrent PC-DOS has evolved in the CP/M environment. DOS programs run either without modification or restriction, with some restrictions, with some modifications, or not at all. A typical restriction may be a program that will run on a color monitor but not on a monochrome monitor.

With a few caveats such as these, most programs run fine. Just because a DOS program is not listed on the documentation list doesn't mean that it won't run. It just means that it may not have been tested. You should try your favorite programs in the Concurrent environment after making sure that you have enough memory to run. You might also check with Digital Research to see if they have added any programs to the list. If your version of Concurrent won't run all the new programs, DRI might have a patch. Check the DR SIG forum on CompuServe for all patches and other technical information.

In the DOS environment, programs never had to worry about memory; they always assumed that they had all of it at their disposal. However, Concurrent must be able to control what each program gets in terms of memory because it must allow other programs to run side by side. Therefore, Concurrent sets a limit on the amount of memory a program may have. Note that this is not a problem for CP/M programs, only for DOS programs. Therefore, for those types of programs that find that they do not have enough space to run in, Concurrent provides two utilities to increase the amount of memory allocated to the program.

For programs that have the .EXE filetype, you use the ADDMEM command. You must use it before loading the program. The allocation you make is good only for that run and in that window. You must use a batch file for each program if you want to increase the allocation every time you load that program. Determine how much additional RAM your EXE program will need and type the command

ADDMEM = n

where n is the additional memory requested. Type ADDMEM alone to display the allocation to verify that it has been granted.

For programs with the .COM filetype, use the COMSIZE command. In order to see the RAM allocation in the current window, type COMSIZE by itself. Determine how much memory your program needs and type that amount. For example, when you need 128K of memory, use

COMSIZE = 128

That will be followed by the verification message

Memory Allocation Size = 128K

This setting, again, is for that run and in that window only. To make it a routine allocation, use a batch file such as

COMSIZE = 128
PROGRAMNAME

When you call this file, it will automatically set your memory to 128K before loading your program.

Programs written under the following versions of CP/M and DOS are the ones under consideration here.

CP/M environment:
 CP/M-86 (not CP/M-80)
 Concurrent CP/M-86 Versions 1.0, 2.0, 3.1
 Concurrent PC DOS

DOS environment:
 PC DOS Version 1.1
 PC DOS Versions 1.0, 2.0 (using Concurrent V4.1)
 PC DOS Version 2.1 (using Concurrent V5.0)

3

GETTING UNDER WAY

Before you can use Concurrent PC DOS, you must install it for use on your computer. Follow the installation routines included in the package for your system. You will be installing Concurrent for use on either a computer with a hard disk (in which case all the files will be copied over to your hard disk) or on a computer with two floppy disk drives. Once you have finished the installation routine, you can start using Concurrent. The following discussion assumes that you have completed the installation procedure since that procedure is unique to each computer.

On a two-floppy-disk machine, turn the computer on and insert the startup disk into drive A and utilities disk 1 into drive B. The computer will take a few moments to go through a diagnostic routine and will then will read a file called CCPM.SYS from the disk in drive A. This file is Concurrent and is loaded into the computer's memory. This process is referred to as loading or booting the operating system. Once Concurrent is loaded, the startup screen shown in Figure 3.1 will be displayed on your computer.

CONFIGURING AN EFFICIENT TWO-FLOPPY CONCURRENT SYSTEM

Because of the size of the Concurrent PC DOS operating system and the large number of utility programs that come with it (not to mention the HELP files and documentation on disk), most users find it useful, if not absolutely necessary, to have a hard disk system. However, you can set up Concurrent

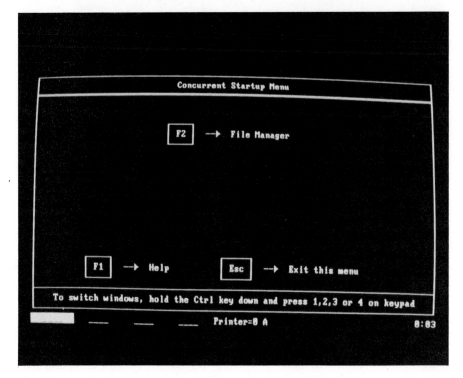

Figure 3.1 Startup Screen for a Two-Floppy System

on a two-floppy (or even a one-floppy) system if you know how, and can then work very efficiently.

The first accommodation that you have to make is that you must be patient enough to switch a few disks as you need them. Obviously, a 360K floppy disk is relatively limited, whereas a 10- or 20-megabyte hard disk seems almost boundless (at first). The next accommodation that you have to make is to understand and use the MDisk feature that Concurrent provides.

This assumes, of course, that you have sufficient RAM memory to utilize MDisk. Concurrent has a minimum memory requirement of 256K. Since the system takes 150K itself, that doesn't leave much room to maneuver. At 512K, you can begin to use the power of concurrency. At higher RAM levels, you can have room for a sizable MDisk as well.

By using an MDisk, you, in effect, take a portion of memory and make it a repository of programs or reference material that you need to use frequently. *Never put valuable data in an MDisk!* Remember, anything put in RAM is volatile and goes away when the power is turned off—or interrupted. A power surge or "spike" will wipe out the contents of RAM and this includes your MDisk. If all you had there was easily replaceable programs and reference material, you have suffered only an annoyance.

However, let's say that you were working in your word processor and "saving" your work on the MDisk instead of a floppy disk. (This can be very fast, hence the temptation.) Along comes a power interruption or a machine glitch and your work is gone! You may have lulled yourself into feeling that you were saving your work, but you weren't. It's as if you were writing it on a chalkboard and while you had your back turned, the janitor erased it.

HOW DO I SET UP AN MDISK?

An MDisk is installed by means of an option under the Concurrent SETUP command. SETUP is menu driven, so you can merely enter the command, press RETURN, and there you are. SETUP gives you seven options to control. However, we will deal only with the MDisk (F4) here. See Digital Research's "Concurrent User's Guide" for information on the other options.

By pressing function key F-4, you enter the routine to set up an MDisk. Once there, you will be further prompted as to the size of MDisk you want to establish. If you have only 256K of RAM, you won't be able to do anything. The system can establish an MDisk only if you have more than the minimum memory. The MDisk will have the characteristics of CP/M media.

Furthermore, you can specify the size and location in memory should you care to do so. You will have to specify size experimentally as you see how much you will need to accommodate your programs or files. As a first approximation, you can add up the file sizes of the programs you want to install (this will probably be bigger than you need). You will want to keep the MDisk as small as possible so that it does not take away valuable RAM and yet keep it large enough to be useful. The minimum size of an MDisk is 32K. By pressing function key F3, you can watch the memory allocation add up (in 16K blocks). You can also see the starting address value lowering. If you press the F5 key, the reverse happens—MDisk shrinks and the starting address rises.

If you picture RAM as a stack of coins, you are marking those coins on the top of the stack for your MDisk; therefore, the "value" of the stack below, decreases—the number goes down. Conversely, if we unmark coins going up the stack, the value increases. An MDisk is usually at the top of memory so as to be "out of the way." If you want to customize your MDisk further, see the "Concurrent PC DOS User's Guide," page 8-92. Once you have set up your MDisk and saved the values in the file CCPM.SYS, it will be there every time that you boot up. Make sure that CCPM.SYS is on the same disk as SETUP and that the disk is not write protected (doesn't have a sticker over the notch).

Other Things That You Can Do

Besides setting up an MDisk, you should also do the following things:

1. Remove all programs and utilities from your working disks that you will not need on a daily basis. Copy them to another disk that you can use

when necessary. The time to do this is when you are making initial backups of your system disks.

2. Make a batch file that contains a command to copy your favorite programs or files (PIP or COPY) onto the MDisk from the floppy at system start-up time.

3. Print out the directory of your system disks and working program and data disks and tape it on the back of each appropriate disk envelope. This will help identify the right disk at the right time and prevent confusion.

CONFIGURING AN EFFICIENT HARD DISK CONCURRENT SYSTEM

If you have a hard-disk-based system with Concurrent installed, simply turn on the computer. Concurrent will be loaded from your hard disk into memory and the Startup Screen will appear.

When the power is on, you can reload Concurrent at any time by holding down the CtRL and AlT (alternate) keys while you press the DeL (delete) key. This CtRL-AlT-DeL combination is referred to as a system reset and causes the computer to reload the operating system from disk (on a floppy-based system, make sure that you return the startup disk and the utilities disk 1 in drives A and B before you attempt this). A system reset will delete any information in memory and will start the system over. The startup screen will be displayed on your computer.

When you are ready to proceed, press function key F1. If you have a hard-disk-based system, Concurrent will respond by displaying the startup menu shown in Figure 3.2.

Concurrent PC-DOS is designed to be very easy to learn and to use. Concurrent still provides a command line interface for the specialist, but rather than forcing you to remember cryptic computer commands, Concurrent displays a series of options on the screen and will allow you to choose from them simply by pressing a function key. This type of system is referred to as a menu-based system. Just as in a restaurant where your dinner choices are presented to you on a menu, Concurrent displays your choices and assigns each of them to one of the 10 function keys. To proceed with any one of your options, you simply press the appropriate function key.

WHAT YOU CAN DO FROM HERE

Once you've started Concurrent and have the startup menu displayed, you can move to the File Manager by pressing function key F2. The File Manager is an easy-to-use, menu-driven system for performing most of the common computer functions. The File Manager is explained in more detail in Chapter 4.

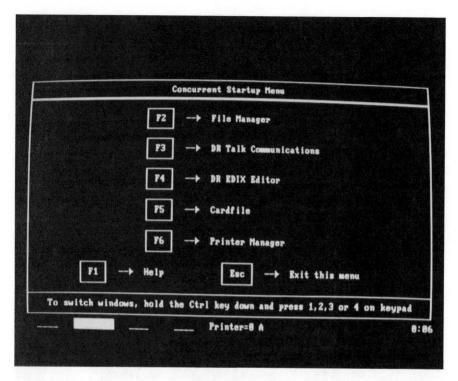

Figure 3.2   Startup Menu for the Hard Disk System

From the startup menu you can also find out more information about using Concurrent by accessing the HELP facility. You can access the HELP facility from any of Concurrent's menus at any time by pressing function key F1. HELP is there to answer any questions you may have while you are using Concurrent. When you access HELP, information relevent to the particular menu you are using is displayed on the screen. When you are finished reading the HELP screen, you return to the menu that you accessed HELP from by pressing the Esc (escape) key. This facility makes it easier to use Concurrent by giving you the information you need when you need it and keeps you from searching through documentation for the relevent information.

If you have installed Concurrent on a hard-disk-based system, the startup menu will include options for DR TALK, a communications program; DR EDIX, a text editing program; CARDFILE, a name and address filing program; and PRINTER MANAGER, a printer control program. By simply pressing the appropriate function key, Concurrent will load and start the selected program. More information on these programs is included in Chapter 6.

Finally, from the startup menu you can exit Concurrent's menu system by pressing the Esc key. When you exit the menu system, Concurrent accepts commands typed in from the keyboard through its command line interface.

While the menu system provides an easy method for using Concurrent's many functions, as you get more familiar with the system you may find typing in commands to be more efficient for accomplishing certain tasks. More information on entering commands from the command line interface is presented in Chapter 4.

STATUS LINE AND WINDOWS

On the very bottom line of your screen, Concurrent displays the status line. The status line continually displays pertinent information regarding how you are using your computer. One of the more important features of the status line is the information it displays regarding Concurrent's windows. When you first load Concurrent, the status line looks as shown in Figure 3.3.

You will notice that the first four entries on the status line are composed of four underlined areas, the first of which is highlighted. The four underlined areas correspond to Concurrent's four windows, and the highlighted portion indicates in which of the four windows you are currently working (called the

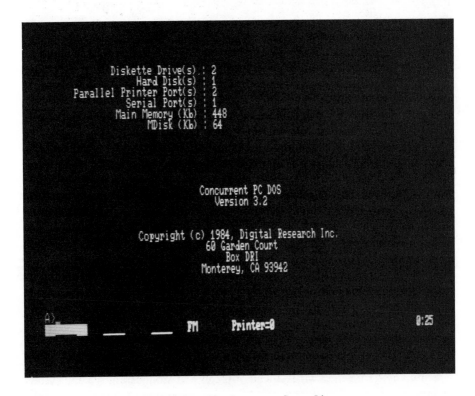

Figure 3.3 The Concurrent Status Line

active or switched-in window). Since the first one is highlighted, you know that you are currently in window 1.

When you switch away from window 1 you are presented with a fresh screen from which you can enter commands or run application programs. Also, the highlighted portion of the status line will change to indicate in which of the four windows you are currently working. This window is now referred to as the active or switched-in window. As you work in any one window, the contents of the other windows remain the same. When you return to the previous window, the contents will reappear exactly as you left it unless you are running a program. If you have left a program running in a window, it will continue processing while you are away using another window (unless you use the SUS-PEND command, discussed in Chapter 10).

The status line will change when you load an application in any of the four windows. For instance, if you load DR TALK in window 1, the status line area that corresponds to window 1 will change from a blank underlined area to the letters "DRTALK." When you load a program into any one of the four windows, Concurrent displays in the status line the name of the file that gets loaded when you start the program. The filename will get displayed in the first, the second, the third, or the fourth position of the status line, depending on which of Concurrent's four windows you used to load the program.

FULL-SCREEN VERSUS PARTIAL-SCREEN WINDOWS

When you start Concurrent, each of the four windows is initially configured to match the full size of your computer's display, or 24 lines by 80 columns. In other words, when you start Concurrent, the entire display is filled with the contents of window 1. If you switch to window 2, the display of window 1 disappears and is replaced by the entire contents of window 2, which then fills the entire display. Window 2 is then referred to as the active window.

When the windows are configured for the full size of your display, or 24 lines by 80 columns, they are referred to as full-screen windows. Initially, all four of Concurrent's windows are configured as full-screen windows. Typically, for most of your work, running your applications in full-screen windows will suffice. The application will appear as it normally does when you run it on a single-tasking system.

Sometimes, though, you may find it more convenient to display portions of two or more windows on the computer's display at the same time. For example, if you start a calculation in one window that you know will take several minutes to finish, you may want to use the time to start writing a letter. However, you may want to monitor the progress of the calculation at the same time. Any time that you wish to see portions of two or more windows at once, you can change any or all of the windows from full-screen windows to partial-screen windows, through the use of the WMENU command.

DOING YOUR WINDOWS

WMENU is called a window manager because it allows you to change the size of any active window, place it somewhere else on the physical screen, copy what is currently on the window screen to a file, and so on. Try the following test. Get to the command line prompt and type in ''WMENU'':

A>WMENU<ENTER>

Concurrent will load the program WMENU into memory and then reissue the command line prompt. The message ''Window Manager Installed'' will appear, but nothing else. WMENU is now reading everything that is typed at the keyboard for this window (you can switch windows and WMENU will not be loaded for that window). It ignores everything except those commands that are directed at it.

How do you get its attention? By typing a Ctrl + (from the keypad, not the uppercase = key). WMENU uses the cursor movement keys on the numeric keypad to select actions in its menu. Once you type Ctrl +, WMENU will replace the status line at the bottom of the screen. What will appear is the menu of operations that WMENU can do. For instance, use the cursor movement keys to move around the WMENU selections (all the cursor keys will work). Move to the window-size option and press <ENTER>.

A new WMENU line will appear indicating the name of the WMENU command and the number of rows and columns in the active window. Now if you hold down the up arrow Key, you should see a double bar move from the bottom of the window to the top. At the same time, the NROWS field will be changing to reflect the new size of the window. The SIZE command will move the bottom and right borders of the window. Using this command you can collapse a window to one character (probably not very useful).

When you are finished sizing the window, press the Esc Key to go back to the main menu (Concurrent uses the Esc Key in exactly the same manner in all its menus.) Once there, select the PLACE option and move the newly sized window to the position you want it to have on the physical screen (again just by using cursor keys on the keypad).

Just for fun, try to set up all your windows so that window 1 is in the top left corner of the screen, window 2 is next to it on the right, window 3 is below window 1, and window 4 is under window 2 (see Figure 3.4).

Even though you have reduced the size of any of the windows, you can expand them to full-screen size by using Ctrl-Del. This combination of keys will flip the currently active window (the one with the flashing visible cursor) between full-screen and partial-screen size. (The WMENU program need not be installed.)

You might also take note that WMENU works on all the windows without you having to install it in each window separately. If you want to change all the window sizes, press Ctrl − + to get the WMENU's attention. Select SIZE

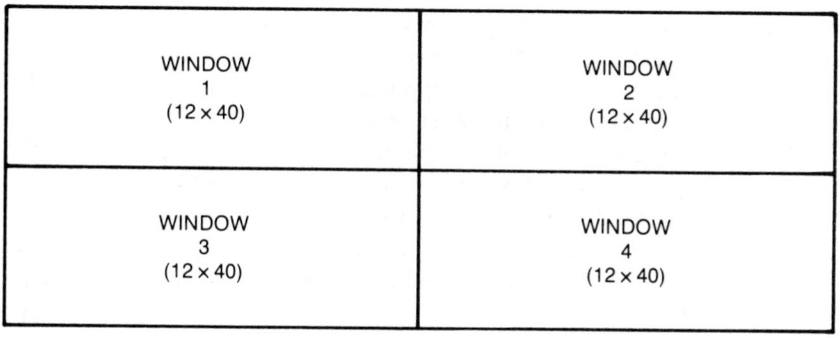

WINDOW 1 (12 × 40)	WINDOW 2 (12 × 40)
WINDOW 3 (12 × 40)	WINDOW 4 (12 × 40)

Figure 3.4 Four Concurrent Windows

and begin to change the sizes of the first or active window. Then switch to the next window you want to change, and so on. When you are finished, use the Esc Key to return to the main WMENU window and either ABORT WMENU or just leave it installed and return to the command line interface by pressing Esc.

Later (Chapter 10) we will discuss some additional things that you can do with WMENU and talk about another windowing function called WINDOW, which provides exactly the same functions as WMENU, but the way you use it makes a big difference. Right now let's just discuss some ideas on how to use windows effectively.

WINDOW USES

Windows are useful for monitoring a number of different tasks. For instance, you can monitor a file being printed from a small window, or keep track of a file transfer program that is receiving or sending a file in the background. If you are connected to a network of other computers, a small window may constantly be displayed to alert you to the status of incoming electronic mail.

Multiple windows can also be used to compare files or data. You can use a split screen, either horizontally or vertically, to display information from two different sources and compare one against the other.

Or if you need to move the contents of one program to another, for example, data from a spreadsheet into a report being written with a word processor, Concurrent's partial-screen windows can prove to be very useful. By displaying portions of the spreadsheet on the screen while you're working on the word processor you can ensure that the data being copied over are accurate. Concurrent also supports a cut-and-paste facility that allows you to read a portion of a window out of one application program and into a text file that can then be read into other application, allowing you to move data between different application programs.

The windows can be fully or partially overlapping. In other words, all or a portion of one window may be placed "on top of" all or a portion of another window, effectively hiding the contents of that window. In a situation where two or more windows are overlapping, the active or switched-in window will always appear on top of the other windows.

If your computer has a color display, WMENU also allows you to alter the colors of the windows. This useful feature allows you to color-code your applications when running two or more these applications in partial-screen windows. You can assign the foreground color (the colors that the characters themselves appear as) and the background color (the color behind the characters) of each window independently.

As you can see, Concurrent's windowing capabilities offer a powerful set of features that are useful in a wide variety of situations. By giving you the ability to view more than one program at a time, Concurrent's windows give you the ability to get the most out of your application programs, even if they weren't originally designed to work together.

SOMETHING TO KEEP IN MIND: SHARED RESOURCES

Being able to run more than one application program at a time is a very powerful feature that, until recently, was available only on large computers. Concurrent's ability to run up to four application programs makes your personal computer act like four computers sitting side by side. To use this feature most efficiently, one very important concept must be kept in mind, the concept of shared resources.

Your personal computer system is made up of a number of components, such as a keyboard, disk drives, a monochrome or color display monitor, and internal memory or RAM. As an application program is loaded and run, that application uses these various components during its execution.

For example, the disk drives are used for reading and writing information to files. The display is used by the application program to present information to you, the user. When you load a program, it requires a certain amount of memory in order to run. These components comprise the major resources needed by that program in order for you to use the program on your personal computer. Each program has its own minimum requirements for most efficient use. The operating system is responsible for managing the demands of the program and ensuring that the computer's resources are utilized as needed.

When you run more than one program at a time, the computer's available resources will have to be shared by the programs. The more programs you run simultaneously, the more Concurrent needs to focus on sharing the available resources among the programs.

Keyboard sharing occurs by having one window always defined as the active window. As you type at the keyboard, the information is routed directly to that active window. To "attach" the keyboard to a program running in another window, you switch the active window using the Ctrl-1, 2, 3, or 4 keystroke sequence.

Concurrent's windowing feature allows you to display portions of two or more programs on your display at the same time. However, certain programs will not allow the display to be shared once they have taken control of the display. These programs are referred to as being "poorly behaved." In these cases, the output of the poorly behaved program will be displayed even after you have switched windows to another program.

Concurrent allows you to run poorly behaved programs on your computer by suspending execution of the program whenever it is no longer in the switched-in or active window. This is referred to as the SUSPEND mode and is discussed in Chapter 11.

4

USING CONCURRENT

THE COMMAND LINE INTERFACE

If you are like most people who use microcomputers, most of the time the computer system will be waiting for you to tell it what to do. It does this by issuing some form of a prompt and then waits for you to respond with a command. This is known as the command line interface. One of the more famous command line interfaces is the "A>" prompt that has characterized the CP/M world for so long, and which is still supported by Concurrent PC DOS.

Here Concurrent PC-DOS displays the drive (such as "A"), a user number if you are somewhere on the disk other than user 0 on CP/M media ("3B" signifies user 3, drive B), and the ">" character that marks the end of the command line prompt. The trick, now, is for you to type in a command and have Concurrent do something.

Each program on your disk is a command that you can ask the computer to run (this includes the utilities that are shipped with Concurrent PC DOS). Most commands require some sort of additional input and expect the input to be given at the same time that you type in the command name. The part of the command that specifies the input is known as the "tail". Thus a command line looks like the following:

A > command tail < ENTER >

The <ENTER> stands for the carriage return or enter key that completes the command line. Following are examples of command lines:

```
A>dir<ENTER>
A>type read.me<ENTER>
A>show [drive,user]<ENTER>
A>sdir [drive=all]*.cmd<ENTER>
```

The first word in each example above represents the command itself. Everything else is part of the command tail. The "*" is a wildcard notation that represents any filename followed by the extension, which in this case is specified by the letters "cmd." Obviously in the first example there is no explicit command tail. That is because Concurrent assumes that what you wanted was a list of all the files in the current directory. Thus there is an implied command tail of *.*. The two wildcard designators in this case represent any filename with any extension. The first example is the same as typing

```
A>dir*.*<ENTER>
```

MULTIPLE COMMANDS ON ONE LINE

Concurrent PC-DOS permits you to enter more than one command at one time. This is useful when you want to batch together several different programs so that the combined execution of the programs results in a logically single act, such as a data base update.

Suppose that you want to go to lunch, but before you go you want to start the data base update, which consists of running three programs, PROGA, PROGB, and PROGC. This combined execution will take some time and you don't want to sit in front of your terminal waiting for one program to finish and then enter the next program to be run. You can build a "batch" or "submit" file that will execute these three programs and treat them as one, or you can enter a multiple command line as follows:

```
A>PROGA ! PROGB ! PROGC<ENTER>
```

Concurrent recognizes the exclamation point as a separator between commands and will first execute PROGA, then PROGB after PROGA is finished, and finally run PROGC after both PROGA and PROGB have finished. Do not confuse this with concurrency. Here we are only forming a convenient linguistic unit to execute three different programs as if they were one. They do not execute at the same time (concurrently), but only after the preceding one has finished. Multiple commands on one line provide a minibatch facility, nothing more.

EDITING COMMANDS

Concurrent also provides some simple command line editing features. If you want to erase a single character, the backspace or delete key erases the last character typed and repositions the cursor (the position on the screen where you are about to type). Control-H has the same effect. Table 4.1 describes what each of the control keys can do.

TABLE 4.1 Control Commands

Control Key	Description
Control-E	Positions the cursor to the beginning of the next line without erasing the previous input
Control-H	Backspaces and deletes one character
Control-I	Goes to the next tab stop
Control-J	Same as using the carriage return or enter key
Control-M	Same as Control-J
Control-R	Redisplays the current line and waits for further input
Control-U	Discards the current line and moves the cursor to the next line
Control-X	Erases the current line and moves the cursor back to the beginning of the line

USING FUNCTION KEYS

With the wealth of commands (or programs) at your disposal, each with its own differing command tails, you can quickly become confused. When using the command line interface you have to know:

1. What to do
2. How to specify the full command, including any options
3. How to specify a command tail

Although this form of user interface is a much faster form of interface, you do have to bring a lot of knowledge to the task. However, Concurrent does supply you with several alternative forms of interface that allow you to do the most common things that you would want to do with either a single function key or with only the movement of the cursor.

The FUNCTION command allows you to ascribe to the various function keys certain commands with complete command tails. The FUNCTION utility is menu driven, which means that it will prompt you to make a selection from a menu of options. It really is quite simple to use since ease of use is a fundamental feature of menu systems. The only thing that you should be aware of is that the string that you type to correspond to the function key can be anything.

If the string is meaningless to Concurrent, it will not be able to do anything and it will tell you so. But you can have Concurrent replace the assigned function key with any text, say the beginning of a command, and let you complete the command.

For instance, suppose that you want to have

sdir[drive = all,user = all]

entered when you press function key F10, and you will supply the file specification yourself. You can do this by not supplying an <ENTER> at the end of the string above when FUNCTION asks you for the text to assign to function key F10. For instance, do *not* use the following instruction:

sdir[drive = all,user = all] < ENTER >

When you have finished specifying a string for each function key you want to program, save your assignments by going back to the main menu and pressing function key F5. This submenu will ask you if you want to save the key assignments in some file other than KEYS.PFK. That's up to you. Remember that each set of function key assignments is applicable only to the window wherein it was made. Thus the function key assignments for window 1 are not used in window 2.

Using the File Manager

Concurrent PC-DOS provides you with a program called the File Manager which can be used to supplant the simple command line interface. The File Manager works on files, but since commands or programs are nothing more than special files, you can view File Manager as another way of executing programs. You can run the File Manager by typing

A > FM < ENTER >

This will invoke the File Manager and fill your console screen with the display shown in Figure 4.1.

READING A FILE MANAGER SCREEN

The screen that the File Manager displays may seem at first glance to be overwhelming. Don't panic. Let's begin to decode it.

The top left-hand corner panel tells you whether your disk is a CP/M or PC-DOS disk and how many free bytes remain on it. Next to this panel is another that tells you the current directory, drive, and if appropriate, the user number.

The large panel in the left center of the screen contains the listing of the files in the directory. We'll call this the object panel.

On the bottom of the screen, the File Manager gives a brief description of what the operation selected does and what each function key is set up to do. Digital Research names this panel the prompt panel.

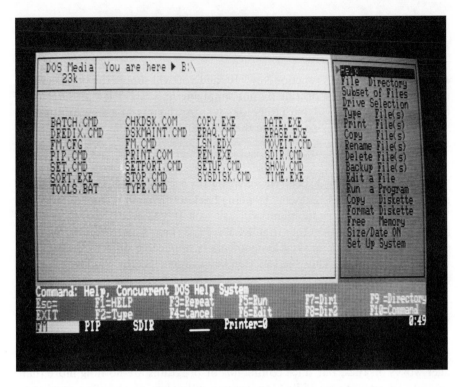

Figure 4.1   File Manager Screen

Finally, on the far right of the screen is a long columnar panel that shows the commands that you can perform on either files, disks, drives, or directories. We'll call this the command panel because these are the operators of the various objects of the system.

The function key descriptions at the bottom of the prompt panel are pertinent only to this menu of the File Manager (the main menu). The function key assignments will change when you select some operation in the command window. However, there is a set of function key assignments that remain fixed no matter what menu you might be in. These assignments are called the Alt-function key assignments (you activate them by pressing the Alt key and the function key at the same time). Table 4.2 lists both sets of key actions. Note that there is some overlap between them.

SELECTING SOMETHING IN THE FILE MANAGER

At this stage the cursor is positioned in the command panel. To move it, press the cursor movement keys (the up/down arrows) to move the cursor up or down (as this is a columnar panel, there is no need to move left or right). Once the

TABLE 4.2 Function Key Descriptions

Function Key	Description
F1	Help
F2	Type
F3	Repeat
F4	Cancel
F5	Run
F6	Edit
F7	Dir 1
F8	Dir 2
F9	Directory
F10	Command
Alt-F1	Help
Alt-F2	Type
Alt-F3	Size/date on/off
Alt-F4	Copy
Alt-F5	Drive C
Alt-F6	Drive D
Alt-F7	Drive A
Alt-F8	Drive B
Alt-F9	Drive
Alt-F10	Command

cursor is where you want it, press <ENTER>. This selects the option, in this case a command. The File Manager highlights the selection by placing it into reverse video mode.

For instance, suppose that you wanted to read a file called READ.ME (that does indeed exist in the current directory). Press the down arrow key four times to position the cursor at the TYPE A FILE option in the command panel (the TYPE A FILE should be highlighted). Pressing <ENTER > selects that operation and the cursor is now positioned at the top left object in the object panel.

Movement in this panel is a little more complicated because it is usually multicolumned. Thus we have to use the left/right arrow movement keys, which work in a manner similar to the up/down keys. Find READ.ME in the list of files and use the cursor movement keys to position the cursor there. Press <ENTER>. Immediately the screen will clear and the contents of the file READ.ME appear on the screen. When you are finished reading the file, Concurrent restores the original File Manager screen with the cursor at the TYPE A FILE option in the command panel.

Another way of selecting either an operation or a file is to type the name of the thing that you want to select. For instance, if you want to delete a file, you could move the cursor to the DELETE A FILE operation, select it with an <ENTER>, and then move to select the filename.

However, the File Manager does permit another way to select. Type the first two characters in the command name "DE" and the File Manager will position the cursor to the delete option and select it for you. To pick the filename, type enough characters to unambiguously identify the filename and then press <ENTER>. As soon as you have specified enough characters to make a selection unambiguously, the File Manager will act on it.

All but one command can be unambiguously selected with at most two characters. Some can be selected with only one character, but COPY   DISKETTE and COPY   FILES need eight characters (there are three spaces between COPY and the rest of the command).

Note that when in the command panel, you will always be able to position the cursor to some selection even when the current cursor position is beyond the item you want to select. In the object window, this is not the case. When the cursor is past the filename that you have tried to select, the File Manager will ask you to position the cursor by using the cursor movement keys or by typing a filename.

Just retype the entire filename or part of a filename that you typed previously and the File Manager will move the cursor to the filename. In other words, the File Manager ignores the first attempt to wrap around the menu. Also note that the File Manager does not select a filename for you once you have specified an unambiguous name as it does in the command panel.

Also observe that if you get what you wanted by typing one character, but there are other commands that begin with that character (i.e., drive selection and diskette maintenance), the File Manager will still look for one more character from the keyboard. Thus, when the File Manager sees the character "D," it moves the cursor to the DRIVE SELECTION option and waits for the next character before selecting (even if you wanted to select a drive). In these cases you either must type in an <ENTER> or type the next character of the command name. Table 4.3 lists the valid abbreviations for the File Manager commands.

In cases where selecting more than one item makes sense (such as copying files from one drive to another), the File Manager uses the Insert key as a selecting device. When the Insert key is struck, the File Manager highlights the selected item but does not act on the selection until the <ENTER> key is pressed. In this way you can choose several files before starting the delete, copy, or rename operations. The Delete key will remove the selected item from the list.

TABLE 4.3   File Manager Commands

Abbreviation	Command
h	Help
f	File directory
fi	File directory
s	Subset of files
su	Subset of files
d	Drive selection
dr	Drive selection
t	Type files
p	Print files
copy f	Copy files
r	Rename files
re	Rename files
de	Delete files
b	Back up files
e	Edit a file
ru	Run a program
copy d	Copy a diskette
fo	Format a diskette
fr	Free memory
si	Size/date on/off
se	Set up system

SPECIAL KEYS IN THE FILE MANAGER

Moving the cursor one position in one direction at a time can get very tedious. Table 4.4 shows the effects of some special keys.

TABLE 4.4   Special File Manager Keys

Key	Description
Home	Return to the top left corner of page 1 of the window
Page Up/Down	Move cursor one page in the specified direction
End	Move cursor to the last entry on the last page of the panel (opposite of HOME)
Tab	Move the cursor between the File Manager panels
Delete	Removes the last selection

TABLE 4.4   Special File Manager Keys (cont.)

Key	Description
Escape	General-purpose stop-what-you-are-doing key (used to exit from the File Manager)
Space	In the command panel, the space bar acts the same as the down arrow key; in the object panel, the space bar acts the same as the right arrow key
Insert	Selects without acting on the selection

COMMENTARY ON THE FILE MANAGER COMMANDS

There are 17 commands available through the command panel. Each is discussed below with any noted side effects.

Help

If you have a color monitor and have set the foreground and background color, you may lose it during execution of HELP through the File Manager. This happens only when the File Manager is started through a menu screen. The colors will be restored when you exit HELP.

There are several ways to return to the File Manager screen. One way is to use the ESC key, while the other is to press <ENTER> when HELP asks you to select a topic. In either case don't become impatient, as it takes a few moments to restore the File Manager screen. Be sure and notice that the function keys have been redefined for HELP. (They will be restored upon exiting HELP.)

Help is context sensitive, which means that if you are trying to back up your files and you need some help, you can press the help function key and get help only on the backup operation. (The HELP function key gives you help only on the subject at hand.)

File Directory

If the disk you are currently working on is a PC-DOS disk, the options for this operation will appear as named subdirectories. If you are using CP/M disks, the options will appear as choices of user numbers.

Subset of Files

If you have a lot of files in your directory, many of them probably don't need to be visible in the object panel. For instance, the various utilities that come with the system can be loaded in the system directory (user 0, system drive). But you probably do not want to see the names of these files but rather any data files that they might work on (especially as there might be 100 or more programs). Therefore, use the SUBSET OF FILES command to filter out any distracting files.

See the comments below about RUN A COMMAND.

Drive Selection

Self explanatory.

Type Files

If you stop the typing of a long file by using the Escape key, the file is still selected but the operation (TYPE A FILE) is not. Thus it is possible to select TYPE A FILE again and immediately start typing the last file selected, something that you probably do not want to do. Before you select another operation, use the Tab key to cross over to the object panel and then press the Delete key to "de-select" the active filename. You may now pick some other operation without automatically using the last filename selected. Of course, there may be some reason for your wanting to have this happen.

If you press any key on the keyboard except <ENTER> or Escape while typing a file, the File Manager will restore the original screen with the filename selected and the cursor in the command panel pointing at HELP.

Print Files

Self explanatory.

Copy Files

Self explanatory.

Rename Files

When you select several files for renaming, the File Manager asks you for a new name to replace each of the old filenames. If the new name already exists, no renaming is done but the selected filename remains selected even after all the other files have been renamed. You may have to "de-select" that file.

Delete Files

The File Manager will always display the selected files for deletion and then request a confirmation before deleting them all.

Backup Files

Backup works a bit differently than the other operations, in that you first have to select the files that you want to back up and then select the BACKUP command.

Edit a File

Self explanatory.

Running a Command

If you have used a wildcard specification to filter the directory display (see SUBSET OF FILES), and then selected RUN A COMMAND, you may encounter some difficulty. If the wildcard specification does not include executable file types, there is nothing appropriate for File Manager to select when asked to do so. In fact, if you select one of the files displayed and it is not executable, an error message will be displayed. You must either reset the wildcard file specification so that executable files appear in the directory panel, or use function key F10, which allows you to type in a command line to Concurrent.

Additionally, you should note that there is no way to specify a command tail when using this operation. If you need to specify a command tail, use function key F10.

Copy Diskette

This operation and the next make use of the DSKMAINT utility, which has a menu interface. However, by selecting this command from the File Manager's command panel, you will not have to descend through all the menu levels of DSKMAINT. You have already gotten beyond those first few menus. The File Manager will locate you at the appropriate place in the menu hierarchy of DSKMAINT. Now when you have to use the Escape key to back out of DSKMAINT to get back to the File Manager, you will have to pass through those menu levels that you avoided upon entry (i.e., you will see more menus on the way out than you saw on the way in).

Format Diskette

Same comments as for COPY DISKETTE.

Free Memory

If you remove the File Manager entry in the memory table, you will not be able to return to the File Manager and will have to invoke it again when you get to the command line interface.

Size/Date On/Off

Self explanatory.

Set Up System

This command makes use of several utilities (SETUP, DSKMAINT,

HDMAINT, FUNCTION, and SETPORT). See the comments for COPY A DISKETTE.

File Manager and FM.CFG

If you have a color monitor, you have the ability to modify the colors used in the File Manager. You do this by creating a file called FM.CFG in user 0 of the system drive. FM.CFG contains the instructions telling the File Manager what colors to use in what panel. There are 16 colors to choose from and four File Manager panels to select. You set the color of the both the characters (foreground) and the screen (background).

There is rigorous syntax that you must adhere to when creating commands in the FM.CFG file. For instance,

$$OBJECT\ FG\ COLOR\ =\ 0$$

means that the foreground color in the object panel is black (the characters in the object panel are black), while

$$OBJECT\ BG\ COLOR\ =\ 2$$

means that the background color in the object panel is red. Thus we would have black characters on a red screen in the object panel.

The syntax is as follows:

$$Panel\ FG/BG\ COLOR\ =\ n$$

where you must specify which panel, whether you want the screen or the characters, and which color. The choices of panels are

$$OBJECT\quad COMMAND\quad PROMPT\quad KEY$$

(KEY refers to the function key assignments at the bottom of the prompt panel.) They must be in uppercase, as well. The choice of colors (n) comes from Table 4.5.

TABLE 4.5 Function Key Color Assignments

n	Color
0	Black
1	Blue
2	Red
3	Magenta
4	Green
5	Cyan
6	Brown

TABLE 4.5   Function Key Color Assignments

n	Color
7	White
8	Grey
9	Light blue
10	Light red
11	Light magenta
12	Light green
13	Light cyan
14	Yellow
15	High intensity white

SUMMARY

In this chapter we have presented two of the three user interfaces: the command line interface and the File Manager. As we could see, the command line interface is really for those of us who have become quite skilled at asking the computer to fetch and carry for us. It requires a lot of recall-type knowledge and some typing skills. Its major defect is that it is not the easiest thing to learn but is acquired through practice and experience.

The File Manager attempts to close the learning gap. By replacing the command line interface with a menu format, it allows for productive use of the computer almost immediately. With the File Manager we do not have to remember commands and their arguments, but how to select the proper command. The File Manager also helps to train us as we become more and more versed in using the Concurrent PC DOS operating system.

In the next chapter we will learn how to write about our menus so that you may construct your own easy-to-use menus tailored to your computing needs.

5

USING THE MENU SYSTEM

This chapter discusses a new user interface: menus. We have already talked about the command line interface and the powerful File Manager interface. Part of the power of the File Manager comes from its use of menus. The command panel of the File Manager is a menu that uses the carriage return or enter key to make selections. Concurrent PC DOS also supplies a facility to create menus that use the function keys to make selections. In this way you can control the amount of information that the user needs in order to execute a program or series of programs.

Before we begin discussing EDITMENU, COPYMENU, and RUNMENU, let's discuss what menus are and how they are stored.

MENU FILES AND MENUS

A menu is stored in a menu file. There may be more than one menu stored in each file. Do not confuse the name of a menu with the name of the file where the menu is stored. Figure 5.1 shows the relationship between menus and a menu file using as an example a series of menus that provide services for floppy disks.

Thus you can put together a series of menus that deal with one type of service, such as maintenance for a floppy disk, and keep them in one menu file. In this case we have one menu file that contains two menus, one that formats a floppy disk and one that provides a copying service for floppy disks.

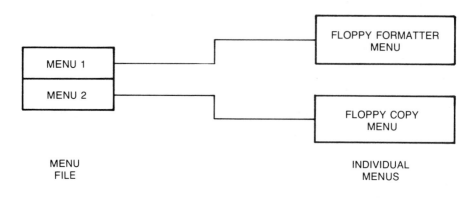

Figure 5.1   Menu Files and Menus

CREATING AND EDITING A MENU

To create a menu, you must use the EDITMENU utility included with Concurrent (Figure 5.2). EDITMENU creates an entry in the menu file and is able to access it when necessary. You cannot use a text editor to do this.

Figure 5.2   EDITMENU Initial Screen

EDITMENU must be given the name of the menu file where the menu exists. For instance,

A>editmenu myfile.dat<ENTER>

If you don't specify a menu file name, EDITMENU (and RUNMENU) will look for a file called MENU.DAT.

When you first create a menu file, EDITMENU will respond by telling you that the file was not found and gives you a choice between creating one or leaving EDITMENU. You may be confused at this point if you have made the mistake of entering the name of the menu instead of the name of the menu file. If you did, exit EDITMENU and start over with the name of the menu file that you wish to create or use, not the name of the menu that you wish to edit within a menu file.

Let's first create a new menu by using the following instructions. Later we will discuss the new concepts that are embedded within this script in greater detail. For this example to work properly, you must test it with SDIR.CMD on the active disk.

MENU CREATION SCRIPT

1. EDITMENU DIR.MNU.
2. Press key F2 to create a new menu file.
3. Press key F2 to create a new menu within DIR.MNU.
4. Enter "direct" as the new menu's name.
5. The screen will clear and the menu editing commands will appear at the bottom, while the top portion will be empty. In the top part of the screen, you can build a menu screen using the functions outlined at the bottom. For the moment we shall build a screen without many of the special editing features.
6. Type "Directory Command Menu."
7. Press key F5 to center the title.
8. Skip five lines (use the <ENTER> key five times).
9. Press the Tab key once.
10. Type "F1," Tab, "Full directory listing, all users/all logged in drives."
11. Skip a line.
12. Type Tab, "F2," Tab, "Directory of all users/drives = ?."
13. Skip a line.
14. Type Tab, "F3," Tab, "Directory of all drives/users = ?."
15. Skip a line.
16. Type Tab, "ESCAPE," Tab, "Return to previous menu."
17. Press key F8 to see how your menu will appear when it is run.

18. Press key F10 to store the menu.

19. Now we must assign function keys to this menu and give them some meaning. The editing screen will disappear and the function key assignment screen will replace it. Enter "A" for the type for F1. This means that the command associated with pressing F1 is a complete command; nothing more is going to be added to the command line. Do not press the <ENTER> key. The cursor will automatically move to the next field in the function key assignment screen.

20. Type "sdir [drive = all,user = all]" in the command text columns. This is the command line that Concurrent PC DOS will execute when key F1 is pressed. Here you must press the <ENTER> key to get to the next line.

21. The cursor is now positioned at the type field of function key F2. Enter "O" as the type, which means that the user must finish the command line.

22. Type "sdir [user = all, drive = ". Because we indicated that this command was incomplete (type 0), Concurrent will display the partial command above on the screen when key F2 is pressed, and wait for you to fill in the rest of the command (when it sees an <ENTER> keystroke, it acts on the command). Type <ENTER>.

23. The type of function key F3 is also "O".

24. Type "sdir [drive = all,user = ".

25. Press key F10 to exit the function key assignment menu.

26. Save the menu and exit to the command line interface.

27. Now we must test our menu. Type RUNMENU DIR.MNU DIRECT to execute the menu we have just created.

EDITING THE MENU

Now that we understand how to create a menu, let's go back to it and add some of the special features that can make a menu a real asset to comprehension. Since we are going to use some color, you may not see any of the changes on the screen if you have a monochrome display.

When dealing with special effects, the special effect exists from one boundary to another. You mark where the special effect is to begin and where it is to end. Thus if you want red letters only in the title, the special characters for red foreground colors must be placed before the start of the title and then at the end of the title.

1. Type at the A> prompt, EDITMENU DIR.MNU <ENTER>. Do not include the name of the menu (DIRECT) on the command line. For some reason EDITMENU gets confused if you do so.

2. Press key F3 to indicate that we want to change an existing menu.

3. When EDITMENU asks for the name of the menu you wish to edit, type "direct."

4. The menu that we have just created will appear in the editing screen with the editing functions on the bottom of the screen. Press key F2. The editing menu at the bottom of the screen will be replaced with a different one. You can move the cursor to any item in the list by using the arrow keys and the space bar. Although the instructions state that the space bar selects an object, that is not the case. The <ENTER> key is the only way to select a special effect. The space bar will act like a cursor movement key, but not a selection key.

5. Select the foreground option.

6. Select the color black. A "˜k" will appear on the screen.

7. You will be out of the special-effects menu and back at the main editing screen. Press key F8 to see the effect of what you have just changed. Obviously, a black foreground color and a black screen will effectively show a blank screen.

8. Now let's set everything to blinking. Press key F2.

9. Select the blink option. The "˜k" should now be "{k."

10. Press key F8 to test the changes. Note that while everything is blinking, we lost the foreground color but retained the character "k" on the screen. This is because when you select a special effect, EDITMENU writes some special character into the menu right where the cursor is pointing. For instance, the special-effect character to indicate the start of the foreground color is "˜." The very next character will be interpreted by RUNMENU as the color code (i.e., "r" for red, "k" for black, etc.). Thus "˜r" results in red characters on the screen until the next ˜x pair (see Table 5.1). At which point a new foreground color will be displayed depends on the value of x. These two characters, "˜r," for instance, are not inserted into the menu screen but replace two characters on the screen. To avoid potential destruction of your menus, you must add enough space in the menu line to allow for any special effect before adding the special effect (use the Ins key). Thus the blink character "{" replaced the foreground color character "˜" in our example.

11. Let's fix the irritating blinking pattern by deleting the blink character and the extraneous "k." Use the Del key to erase the character at which the cursor is pointing (a "{"). As this will remove a character from the title (a space), use the Ins key to add the missing space.

12. Now let's brighten all the function key items in the menu (F1, F2, F3, Esc). This will make them stand out from the rest of the menu. Move to the cursor position in front of the "F1" item. (This is because when we add the brighten character we want to replace the space in front of the "F," not the "F" itself.)

13. Press key F2.

14. Select the bright option. A "}" should appear on the screen just before the "F1".

15. Move to the space just after the "F1".

16. Press key F2.

17. Select the bright option. The "F1" menu item should be sandwiched with "}".

18. Press key F8 and preview the new screen. You will note that the characters "F1" will appear much brighter than the others on the screen.

19. Now using the same technique, add the brighten special characters to the other function selection items on the menu screen (F2, F3, Esc). As a short-cut, you do not have to enter the special-effects menu to get a special effect. Now that you know several of the characters that the menu system recognizes in order to create special effects, you just have to use that character. In this case just add the character "}" before and after the F2, F3, and Esc menu items.

20. Finally, let's put the title in reverse video. Move to the beginning of the screen using the Home key.

21. Move to the first space just in front of the title.

22. Press key F2.

23. Select the reverse video option. A "\" should appear on the screen in front of the title.

24. Move to the first space at the end of the title and add a reverse video special-effect character (\). If you don't, the entire screen will be placed in reverse video mode. Test this by using the F8 preview key before adding the closing reverse video character.

25. Let's add a border of diamonds to this menu. This will require the use of another special effect, the special characters. These are graphics characters that your computer can reproduce. First position the cursor to the place where you want to add a special character; you will not be able to move about on the menu screen without adding a special character, once you select the graphics characters in the special-effects menu.

26. Position the cursor to the top left-hand corner of the screen (Home).

27. Insert two lines by using key F3 twice.

28. Press key F9.

29. The lower screen should now be replaced with the special graphics character menu. Move the cursor to the character you want by using the cursor movement keys. Some of the function keys have been redefined so that they add the selected character to the screen in special ways. F7 adds the character and then positions the cursor to the spot just above the previous cursor location (moves up the column). F8 moves down the column. F9 moves along the row from right to left, while F10 moves along the row

from left to right. Select the diamond character (the fourth character from the left on the top special-character row).

30. Hold key F10 down until you have added the diamond character all along the first row. Try to stop when the cursor reaches the first position in the next line. If you cannot stop in time, don't worry. All this means is that you will have to clean any extra diamonds and position the cursor at the first column, second row. Unfortunately, you will have to escape to the editing screen menu, make the changes, and then come back to the special-character menu.

31. We should add one row of diamonds with the cursor sitting at the first position of the second line. Use key F8 to add the leftmost border until you get to three rows below the Esc menu item.

32. Now use key F10 to build the bottom border. Try not to go past the last row, as we want to create the rightmost border by traveling up from the bottom border to the top border.

33. With the cursor in the last column of the row, use key F7 to build the right border.

34. Press key F8 and test your work.

35. Press key F10 to finish with the editing screen menu.

36. As we don't need to reassign any of the function keys, press key F10 and save this menu. Use Esc to exit EDITMENU.

37. Try RUNMENU DIR.MNU DIRECT < ENTER> to play with our little menu.

TABLE 5.1   Special Effects and Color Codes

Character	Description
\	Reverse video
–	Underline (for monchrome displays)
}	Bright
{	Blinking
|x	Sets background to color x starting at the position of the |
|X	Sets the background to color X starting at the position of X; note the difference in upper- versus lowercase in the last special character
`x	Sets the foreground color to x
b	Blue
c	Cyan
g	Green
k	Black
m	Magenta
r	Red
w	White
y	Yellow

MORE ON ASSIGNING FUNCTION KEYS

As we saw in our first script, after we have built a menu we need to associate a meaningful command string that is sent to Concurrent when we press the appropriate function key. For instance, in our example when we press key F1, the command

sdir [drive = all,user = all]

is sent to Concurrent. Thus every time we finish creating or editing a menu, EDITMENU will ask us to assign commands to the function keys. This is similar to the action of FUNCTION.

Each function key assignment has a type associated with it. In our example we used two types, A and O, which represent complete commands and commands needing further instructions, respectively. (The result of not specifying the rest of the command tail when using the O type is dependent on the command.) Table 5.2 shows all the command types.

TABLE 5.2   Associated Command Types

Type	Description
A	Complete command
O	Incomplete command; user enters more
M	Name of another menu in this file
C	User enters entire command line
E	Exit
Blank	No command is associated

Let's play with another type that will be very important to you as you begin to develop sophisticated menus. Although our example is not very sophisticated, it does suffice to demonstrate how to use the M type (or how to build hierarchical menus). For another example of a utility that uses this type of menu that calls another menu, see DSKMAINT.

THE FINAL SCRIPT

1. Let's edit our menu DIRECT. Type EDITMENU DIR.MNU <ENTER> at the system prompt.
2. Press key F4 to copy the old menu to another menu. This is a precautionary measure and can be skipped. However, it does expose us to another feature of EDITMENU.
3. Enter "direct2" as the name of the new menu, and "direct" as the name of the old menu. EDITMENU will copy DIRECT to a new menu called DIRECT2 within the menu file DIR.MNU.

4. The original menu screen should appear. Choose F3 to edit the new menu DIRECT2 (we must make our changes).

5. Insert a new line to the menu that reads as follows:

F4   Show space on drives

Make sure that you highlight the F4 characters.

6. Since we added a new line to the system, you'll have to remake the diamond borders. The new menu screen should look as shown in Figure 5.3.

7. Press key F10 when you have finished adding the new menu selection.

8. The function key assignment menu should now appear. Use the Tab key to move through the type and command sections until you get to the first unused function key field, F4. If you make a mistake and go beyond, use the shift Tab to go backward until you come to the type field of key F4. Enter "M" for the type for F4 and "SPACE" for the command. A type M means that RUNMENU will look in the current menu file (DIR.MNU) for the menu SPACE and display it on the screen.

9. Press key F10 to exit this part of EDITMENU and save the new menu.

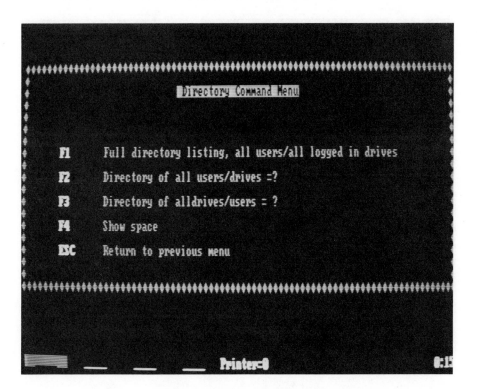

Figure 5.3 Picture of New Menu

10. Now we must construct the new menu SPACE. Press key F2 to select the new menu choice. Enter "space" as the name of the new menu.

11. Now that you are in the main editing screen of EDITMENU, enter the menu that you want to see when you press key F4 when running the DIRECT menu. Use Figure 5.4 as an example. For the sake of brevity, I have not included any special characters in this menu. However, don't feel constrained; have some fun.

12. When you have finished editing that menu, press key F10 to get us to the function key assignment screen. For the example in Figure 5.4, F1 is a type A with a command line of

>   show

and F2 is a type A, also with a command line of

>   show [drive]

13. Press key F10 and save this menu. Exit EDITMENU.

14. Test this new menu that calls another menu that calls another menu by typing RUNMENU DIR.MNU DIRECT2. Press key F4 and see if our

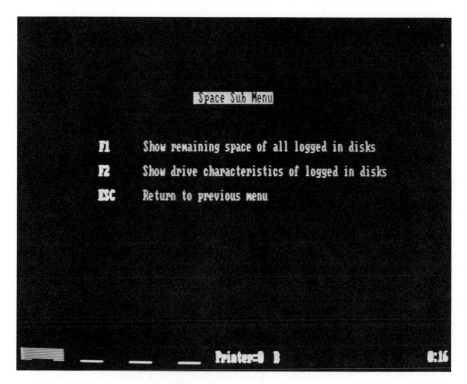

Figure 5.4   Space Sub Menu Screen

second-level menu appears and works as desired. (You can always test these kinds of menus by typing in the command that you wanted to be executed at the press of a function key.)

LAST THOUGHTS

At the bottom of the function key assignment menu appears a reference to pressing key F2 and disabling <ENTER>, and so on. This may be confusing at first sight. However, there are forces at work, Dr. Watson, that would give stout men pause. Suppose that you want to prevent the user from ever escaping the confines of the menu system that you build and getting into the command line interface of Concurrent (a work environment where a user only needs/wants a text editor and some printing facilities). However, the Esc key allows the user to leave the menu when it is at the top level. For instance, in our first menu, DIRECT, pressing the Esc key gets us back to the command line interface, whereas if we pressed the Esc key when we were at the level of the SPACE menu, we would only go back one level, back to DIRECT2.

EDITMENU will ask you to make some determinations concerning these types of issues if you press key F2 in the function key assignment screen. It does this by asking yes/no-type questions about:

1. Disabling the Esc key.
2. Preventing the user from entering commands other than those in the menu list. (Pressing <ENTER> will normally allow the user to enter a command.)
3. Allowing a change in the drive or user number to remain in effect. If the menu selection involves a change in the drive or user number, do you want that change to be in effect after the user moves out of that menu?
4. Any commands to run just prior to or just after the execution of the menu hierarchy.

These additional parameters are saved along with the menu and the function key assignments and associated commands when you elect to save the menu.

Be careful if you decide to disable the Esc key. This is the only way that a user has to get out of the menu system. Take a look at the E type of command and note that it allows the user to exit back to the operating system. Therefore, you might want to leave yourself a backdoor if you decide to eliminate the Esc key route. Of course, this may defeat the purpose you intended. (STOP doesn't work because RUNMENU is a built-in command and doesn't exist on its own. Thus there is no other process to stop.)

6

CONCURRENT PC DOS APPLICATIONS

Concurrent PC DOS comes equipped with a number of applications that enable you to make greater use of your computer operating system. These applications include:

CARDFILE: electronic address book program

DR TALK: communications program

DR EDIX: text editor

BACK/REST: hard disk backup and restore program

PRINTER MANAGER: control for printing activities

In this chapter we discuss the various attributes of these programs.

CARDFILE

Cardfile turns your computer into an electronic address book. Like the address book, Cardfile lets you keep track of names, addresses, and phone numbers of friends or business acquaintances in an organized manner.

However, since it can use the power of a computer, Cardfile has additional features that make keeping track of your contacts much more efficient. For example, you can search for a listing by either first name, last name, business name, or phone number. Cardfile also lets you print out a single list or the entire contents of your address book. Either the complete contents of each list (including phone number and comments) can be printed or just the name and address of the list for mailing labels.

Since Cardfile is designed to work with Concurrent PC DOS multitasking and windowing features, you can have your address book always available in another window and just a keystroke away. For instance, while you are in the middle of writing a letter using a word-processing program, you can call up Cardfile in another window to find the correct address. Or you can have Cardfile print out mailing labels of all your customers while still using your computer for other tasks.

Starting Cardfile

You can start Cardfile in one of three ways:

1. Enter "CARDFILE" from Concurrent's command line prompt. If you have a color monitor on your system, enter "CARDFILE COLOR."
2. Use the "RUN A PROGRAM" command from Concurrent's File Manager and select the file CARDFILE.CMD.
3. Pressing key F5 from Concurrent's startup menu if you have a hard-disk-based computer.

When you start Cardfile, the screen shown in Figure 6.1 appears.

Cardfile is organized around a series of index cards that contain name and address information. Each entry you put into Cardfile will have a unique card associated with that entry. Each card contains fields for the name, business, street address, city, state, zip code, and telephone number. Additionally, Cardfile includes fields for the first name and for a short comment about the individual or company.

Beneath the cards are three lines. The third line is the prompt line, which will prompt you for the appropriate action when specific commands are invoked.

Certain commands will require you to provide additional information. For instance, when you specify SEARCH you will have to provide the name you wish to search for. The second line will be used to enter the additional information when appropriate. The first line lists the Cardfile commands. When you start Cardfile the first command, SCROLL, is highlighted. To indicate to Cardfile which command to perform, you must first point at the command using the left arrow and right arrow cursor movement keys or by using the space bar to step from one command to the next. Each command in turn is highlighted as you point at it. Once you point at the appropriate command, select it by pressing <ENTER>. Cardfile will then execute that command.

Scrolling

Press the up arrow or down arrow cursor movement keys to display the next card in that direction. When you reach the final card, Cardfile will automatically start again back at the first card.

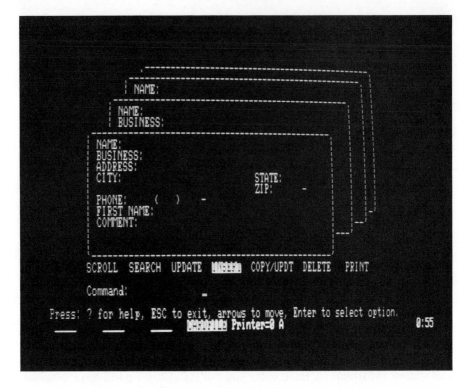

Figure 6.1 Initial Cardfile Screen

You can continuously scroll through the entire contents of Cardfile by selecting the SCROLL command. When you select the SCROLL command, Cardfile will start automatically scrolling through its contents, one card at a time. Pressing the up arrow or down arrow cursor movement keys will reverse the direction of the scroll. Pressing any other key will stop the scrolling.

The SEARCH Option

When you select the SEARCH option, Cardfile gives you a choice of searching on the name, phone number, first name, or business field. Cardfile then prompts you to type in the information you wish to search for.

Cardfile will display the closest match to the specified information. If you wish to see additional cards in the file, use the up arrow and down arrow cursor movement keys to scroll through the nearby cards.

Updating Information on a Card

When you need to update information on a card, for instance, when a phone number changes or an acquaintance moves, first find the appropriate card using either the SEARCH or SCROLL feature. When the correct card is displayed, select the UPDATE command.

Once you have selected UPDATE, the cursor will move to the first character in the name field. You can update any information on the displayed card by simply typing over it. Pressing the <ENTER> key will move you from field to field. When you are through updating the information, press the Esc key. If you wish to save the updated information, respond YES to the Cardfile prompt and press <ENTER>.

Inserting a New Card

The INSERT command allows you to enter a new card to the file. INSERT presents you with a blank card and positions the cursor to the first character of the NAME field. Type in the appropriate information, moving between the fields by pressing <ENTER>.

When you have finished entering the new information, press Esc. Cardfile then asks you if you wish to save the information. Select the YES or NO response using the cursor arrow keys and press <ENTER>. If you answer YES, Cardfile will save the card in its proper alphabetic location and will wait for your next command.

Copying and Updating a Card

The COPY/UPDT command is like the UPDATE command discussed earlier. However, the COPY/UPDT function first makes an identical copy of the selected card, allowing you to update one version while still keeping an unchanged copy. This feature is convenient for maintaining both a home and a work address for one person, or for maintaining cards for two or more people at the same work address and phone number.

When you select COPY/UPDT, the duplicate card is presented. Fill in the card and save it according to the directions given in the UPDATE command described above.

Deleting a Card

The DELETE command removes the displayed card from Cardfile. To help prevent accidental deletions, Cardfile displays the following prompt to allow you to confirm your action:

Remove?   NO   YES

If you select YES, Cardfile will delete the displayed card. If you select NO, Cardfile will leave the card and wait for your next command.

Printing Cards and Mailing Labels

The PRINT command will print either the entire contents of the displayed card, just the name and address for a mailing label, one card at a time, or print all the cards contained in Cardfile.

When you select the PRINT command, Cardfile prompts you to select the desired action. If you select one of the PRINT ALL options, the entire contents are printed. At any time you wish to stop the continuous print function, press the Esc key.

Getting HELP

You will find Cardfile to be a very straightforward program that is extremely easy to use. Prompts are presented throughout Cardfile that explain what action you can take next. Cardfile also includes an on-line HELP function that you can get by pressing the Home key. Pressing Home will display most of the features of Cardfile.

Exiting Cardfile

To exit Cardfile, press the Esc key. Cardfile will ask you to confirm with the following prompt:

Exit?   NO   YES

Select YES using the Cursor Movement keys and press <ENTER>. However, since Cardfile is a handy program to have around, you may wish to keep it constantly running on one of Concurrent's windows.

What Cardfile Requires

During its execution, Cardfile will use the following files.

CARDFILE.CMD	Program file that is loaded when you start Cardfile
CARDFILE.DIS	Contains display information
CARDFILE.DAT	Data file
CURRENT.TRM	Contains information pertaining to color and monochrome monitor displays
NAME.IDX	Data file indexed by name field
PHONE.IDX	Data file indexed by phone number field
FIRST.IDX	Data file indexed by first name field
BUSS.IDX	Data file indexed by business field

Cardfile will start with only the CARDFILE.CMD, .DIS, and .TRM files. Cardfile will automatically create blank .IDX and CARDFILE.DAT files,

resulting in no cards being present. In order to load, Cardfile requires 128k
of available memory.

DR TALK

The computer is a very useful tool for manipulating almost any kind of information. Information may be on a floppy disk, hard disk, tape, or you might
have to type it in manually. Sometimes the information may also be stored on
another computer.

If the two computers are close enough and can read each other's floppy
disk, you could transfer information on a floppy. However, it is often the case
that the two computers have different ways of writing the data on a floppy,
and what is readable on one machine is garbage on another. And what if the
two computers are not conveniently close by?

DR TALK was designed to allow one computer to talk to another. DR
TALK provides a link between a microcomputer and another microcomputer,
a microcomputer and a main frame computer, your computer and a bulletin
board or data base service, and so on.

For instance, a branch office can keep track of its expenses locally on its
personal computer. Once a week the information can be sent to the corporate
computer, where it can be combined with expense information from all other
branch offices, which in turn can be transmitted back to all the branches.

How Communications with DR TALK Works

To communicate between two computers, the systems need to be physically
connected in some manner. This could simply be via a cable hooking the two
computers together. However, most often the computers are connected over
standard telephone lines using a modem.

For the two computers to communicate, they need to follow a standard
set of rules or protocol. For instance, when you want to send a file to a remote
computer, that computer better be waiting to receive the file. DR TALK controls the protocol of the conversation, including dialing up the phone over the
modem to connect with the other computer, sending information over the phone
line, receiving information, and storing it in a file or hanging up the telephone
line when your session is finished.

Starting DR TALK

You can load DR TALK in one of three ways:

1. By entering "DRTALK" from Concurrent's command line prompt
2. By using the "RUN A PROGRAM" command from Concurrent's File
   Manager and selecting the file DRTALK.EXE

3. By pressing key F3 from Concurrent's startup menu if you have a hard-disk-based computer

When DR TALK starts, the following message, along with identifying information, appears on your screen:

$$= = = \text{Proceed} . . .$$

At this point DR TALK is waiting for your command.

Dialing up Another Computer

If you have an acoustic-coupler-type modem, dial the phone number and place the telephone headset in the modem cradle. Switch the modem to data mode. After you've made the connection you are now ready to communicate with the computer.

If you have a direct-connection-type modem, you can send commands to dial directly from the keyboard. This is accomplished from DR TALK's dialing directory. To get to the dialing directory, hold down the Alt key on your

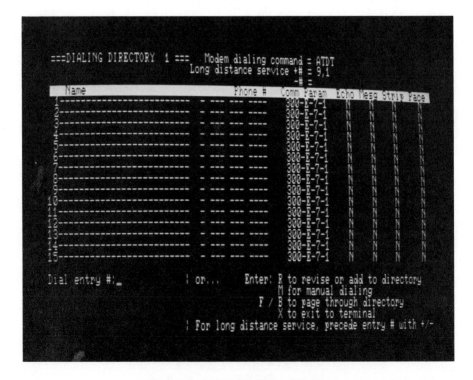

Figure 6.2 DR TALK Dialing Directory

keyboard and press D. Figure 6.2 shows a sample dialing directory. The first time you call up the dialing directory, all entries are blank.

The prompt

Dial entry #

indicates that you can now specify a number to dial or you can select one of the options presented on the lower right-hand portion of the screen.

Dialing can take place either manually or automatically. If you have already stored phone numbers in the dialing directory, you can select a phone number to dial by typing the entry number you wish to dial and pressing <ENTER>.

To dial manually, type M and press the <ENTER> key. You will be prompted for the phone number to be dialed. Type in the phone number (just type in the digits; do not type in brackets around the area code or dashes or spaces within the phone number) and press <ENTER>.

When the dialing is complete and if the connection is successful, you can now start entering commands to the remote computer. The commands you type at the keyboard will appear on your screen but are ignored by your local computer. The commands are transmitted to the remote computer for execution. Responses from the remote computer will be displayed on your screen.

If the commands you type do not appear on your computer screen, hold down the Alt key and press E. This command will cause your computer to display the commands on your screen as you type them in. As before, they will still be transmitted to the remote computer. Typing Alt-E again will toggle this echo feature off.

Changing and Adding to the Dialing Directory

When you first load DR TALK the dialing directory includes no entries and displays the flashing cursor next to the prompt:

Dial entry # :__

To change or add information to the directory, type R and press the <ENTER> key at the prompt. Next, specify the number of the entry you wish to update or add. You will be prompted to enter the name (up to 20 characters) and the phone number (up to 36 characters) to be assigned to that entry.

Next, DR TALK will ask you if the communications as currently defined by DR TALK (referred to as communications parameters) are acceptable. The communication parameters define the protocol by which different computers communicate with one another. The parameters used by DR TALK are set for the most common type of computer communications and should be sufficient for most of your sessions. Type Y to indicate that the default parameters are acceptable.

For an in-depth discussion regarding the various communication parameters, refer to the Concurrent PC DOS User's Guide. Also, refer to the documentation included with your modem for any specific communications settings required by the manufacturer.

Receiving and Saving Information in a File

At any time, whatever appears on your screen can be stored in a disk file for future use through the SCREENDUMP function. Invoke SCREENDUMP at any time by holding down the Alt key and pressing S. This stores the entire contents of the screen, together with the time and the date, in a file called SCRNDUMP.PCT. The file is a standard Concurrent PC DOS file and can be viewed, copied, or deleted like any other file. If you wish to store the contents of the screen again at a later time, simply press Alt-S again; the current time, date, and the contents will be APPENDED to the end of the SCRNDUMP.PCT file. This feature allows you to selectively store portions of your communication session for later review.

Sometimes you may wish to save an entire DR TALK session, instead of saving a screenful at a time. Turn on the receive function by holding down the Alt key and pressing R, or by pressing the PgDn key. You will be asked to type in a drive and a file name in which to save the contents of your session. Alt-R or PgDn can be activated at any time within the DR TALK session.

After you have enabled the receive function, everything that appears on the screen will be routed to the file that you have specified. Both the information that you type and the information that is sent back from the remote computer will be routed to the designated file. To remind you that the receive function is activated, the name of the receiving file is displayed at the bottom of your console.

You can terminate the receive function by pressing Alt-R or PgDn again. The keystroke acts like a toggle; if the receive function is off, pressing Alt-R or PgDn turns it on. If the receive function is on, pressing Alt-R or PgDn turns it off. To prevent accidental erasures of files, if you specify the name of an existing file when prompted for the receive file, all information will be appended to the end of that file.

Sending Information to a Printer

Just as you can route portions of your session to be saved in a disk file, you can route either a screenful of information or your entire session to a printer. To send the contents of your screen to the printer, hold down the Shift key and press the PrtSc key. Ensure that the printer is connected and properly functioning before pressing Shift-PrtSc.

For continuous output to the printer, hold down the Ctrl key and press PrtSc. The following message will appear on the screen:

$$= = =PRINTOUT\ ON= = =$$

From this point on, all information that appears on your computer's screen will be routed automatically to the printer. To terminate this function, press Ctrl-PrtSc again. When you do this, the following message will appear on your screen:

$$= = =PRINTOUT\ OFF= = =$$

At this point, no other information will be routed to the printer unless the Shift-PrtSc or Ctrl-PrtSc sequence is pressed again.

Transmitting a File

To transmit a file to the remote computer, hold down the Alt key and press T. When prompted for the name of the file to transmit, type in the complete name of the file and press <ENTER>. The contents of the specified file will appear on your screen while being transmitted, and the name of the file will be displayed on the bottom of the screen.

At any time during the transmission you can cancel the function by pressing Alt-T again. Transmission will terminate normally when the complete file has been sent.

Assigning Definitions to Keys

One of the most useful features of DR TALK is the ability to assign a series of characters to a single keystroke. Often you will find yourself repetitively typing in the same string of characters over and over. Passwords, commonly used filenames, and data base service commands are just a few of the examples of character strings that you may have to enter several times during one communication session.

Rather than typing in a long series of characters over and over, you can simply assign it to either a function key or to an Alt-number combination. At any time by pressing the assigned key, the entire string will be transmitted.

You can assign a character string to each of the function keys F1 through F10, the combination of Alt-F1 through F10, Shift-F1 through F10, and Ctrl-F1 through F10, making a total of 40 character string assignments. Each assignment can be up to 126 characters long.

To assign characters to a function key, first display the function key directory by holding down the Alt key and pressing K. The first time you display the function key directory all entries will be blank. A sample function key directory with several entries already included is displayed in Figure 6.3

The function key directory will first display the assignments to Keys F1 through F10. Even though each key can contain up to 126 characters, only the

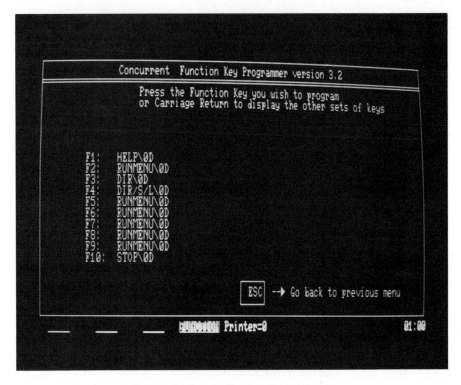

Figure 6.3 Sample Function Key Directory

leftmost 30 will be displayed. As you enter more than 30 characters, the contents will scroll to allow you to enter more characters.

Press F to page forward to see the assignments to the Alt-F1 through F10, Shift-F1 through F10, and Ctrl-F1 through F10 keys. Pressing B will page back through the assignments.

Press R to assign a character string to any of the displayed keys or to revise a current assignment. You will be prompted to type in the number of the key you wish to define and then for the character string you wish to assign. Press <ENTER> to return to the main function key directory. From here you can exit the function key directory by typing the character X.

If you wish to include the <ENTER> key within a character string, type the right curly bracket "}" where you wish the <ENTER> key to be.

These assignments are stored in a file named DRTALK.KEY. Every time you start DR TALK, this file is read and the function keys will be assigned accordingly. If DRTALK.KEY is not present when you start DR TALK, a new one is created with blank assignments to all the function keys.

Temporary Key Definitions

The function key assignments referred to in the preceding section are permanent since the assignments are loaded every time DR TALK starts. You can temporarily assign 10 additional character strings to the Alt-1 (hold down Alt and press 1) through Alt-0 (hold down Alt and press 0) keystroke sequences. You specify which of the 10 you wish to assign by holding down the Alt key and pressing = . This displays a prompt at the bottom of your screen, asking for the key you wish to define. Respond by pressing any of the 10 keys from 1 to 0.

You will then be prompted to enter the character string to be assigned to that Alt combination. You may specify up to 50 characters to be assigned to the string. When you have specified the complete string, terminate the definition by typing <ENTER> . DR TALK will display the first seven characters of the Alt-key assignments on the last line of the screen. These Alt definitions are not saved and are lost when you exit DR TALK. If you wish to save a character string from one DR TALK session to the next, use the function key definitions as outlined in the preceding section.

Exiting DR TALK

When you are finished with your communications session and you wish to exit DR TALK, hold down the Alt key and press X. This will exit from DR TALK and return you to Concurrent PC DOS.

Additional DR TALK Features

DR TALK includes a number of other important and useful features. Table 6.1 outlines a few of the more useful commands.

TABLE 6.1   DR TALK Commands

Command	Description
Alt-C	Clears the contents of the screen
Home	Pressing the Home key displays a list of all DR TALK commands
Alt-V	Prompts for a filename, and displays the contents of that file on the screen
Alt-Y	Prompts for a filename and deletes that file from the disk
Alt-P	Displays and allows changes to the current communications parameters
Alt-F	Displays and allows changes to the program defaults
Alt-Z	Displays the elapsed time for the current communications session

What DR TALK Requires

During its execution, DR TALK will use the following files.

DRTALK.EXE   This is the program file that is loaded into memory when you start DR TALK.

DRTALK.DIR   Contains the information for the dialing directory

DRTALK.KEY   Contains the information for the function key assignments

DRTALK.DEF   Contains the default characteristics for DR TALK

If DRTALK.DIR, DRTALK.KEY, or DRTALK.DEF are not present when you try to start DR TALK, new, planned versions will be created automatically by DR TALK. Whatever settings you had previously stored in the dialing directory, the function key menu or any changes you made to the program defaults will not be included.

DR TALK requires 128K of available memory in order to be used.

DR EDIX

One of the more popular uses of personal computers is as a tool for writing memos, letters, or reports. Using a computer as a word processor offers a number of advantages over using a typewriter or pad of paper and a pencil. Correcting mistakes or changing part of your text becomes much faster and easier. Rather than retyping the whole document because of a misspelled word, you can simply delete the word on your computer's screen and retype the correct one.

DR EDIX is a text editing program that is designed to allow you quickly and easily to compose documents, reports, letters, and memos. A major feature of DR EDIX is its ease of learning and ease of use. A HELP screen that gives you further assistance on how to use DR EDIX is always just a keystroke away. At any time during your session, you simply press function key F7 to reach HELP.

Besides being easy to use, DR EDIX includes a number of features not commonly found in text editors. You can split your computer's display into windows in order to view or compare the contents of various files. While similar in concept to Concurrent's windows, DR EDIX's windows are separate and independent. The entire DR EDIX session, including its windows, takes place in one of Concurrent's four windows.

DR EDIX also contains a tutorial that teaches you the basic information on how to use the program. The tutorial can help you get started using DR EDIX in a very short time. To start the tutorial from the command line prompt, simply type "STUDENT" and press the <ENTER> key or use the "RUN A

PROGRAM'' command from the File Manager to execute the STUDENT.BAT file. The tutorial is interactive and will tell you how to proceed.

DR EDIX commands are initiated by holding down the Ctrl or Alt keys and simultaneously pressing one character. Additionally, the function keys are redefined by DR EDIX to take on special meanings when using the program.

Starting DR EDIX

You can load DR EDIX in one of three ways:

1. By entering "DREDIX" from Concurrent's command line prompt
2. By using the "RUN A PROGRAM" command from Concurrent's File Manager and selecting the file DREDIX.CMD
3. By pressing function key F4 from Concurrent's startup menu if you have a hard-disk-based computer

When you start DR EDIX, the screen presented in Figure 6.4 will appear. The last two lines of the DR EDIX screen are referred to as the status area. The status area displays information pertaining to your session while you are

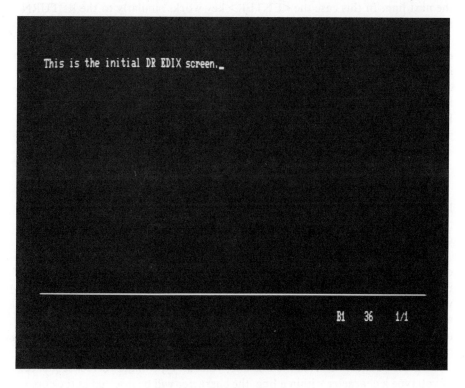

Figure 6.4   DR EDIX Screen

using DR EDIX. At various times filenames, row or column numbers, or prompts requesting information will appear in this area.

The first 21 lines of the DR EDIX screen are referred to as the text area and are separated from the status area by a horizontal line. When you start DR EDIX the text area is initially blank, and the flashing cursor will appear in the upper left-hand corner of the screen. The text area is the blank "piece of paper" where you write your document. To start writing your document, simply start typing as you would on a typewriter.

Composing a Memo

The blank "piece of paper" that DR EDIX works with is up to 254 displayable characters wide, and depending on how much memory you have available, can be hundreds of lines long. At any one time, you can see only the 21 lines by 80 characters that are displayed in the text area of the screen. If you type more than 80 characters on one line, the screen will start scrolling horizontally to continue displaying the information as you type. At any time you can finish typing on one line and move to the next line down by pressing the <ENTER> key. <ENTER> will move the cursor to the first character in the next line. In this case the <ENTER> key works similarly to the RETURN key of a typewriter.

The ability to work on text wider than the 80 columns of your computer's display is a major feature of DR EDIX. Many computer printers can print out in wider formats. Although for most documents, 80-character lines will be sufficient, sometimes you may wish to edit wider formats. For instance, you may have a financial worksheet containing a full year's worth of information to edit. Having lines longer than 80 characters allows you to space the information across the line for clarity of the final printed report.

Correcting a Mistake

If you make a mistake while typing, you can erase by using the backspace key. Pressing the backspace key moves the cursor one space to the left and deletes the character. If the mistake were made earlier in the body of the text, you can erase the mistake using the Del key.

Simply use the arrow keys to move the cursor around the screen. Pressing one of the arrow keys moves the cursor one space in the direction indicated: up, down, left, or right. Once the cursor is directly underneath the character you wish to delete, press the Del key. The character above the cursor will disappear and the rest of the line to the right of the cursor will shift one space to the left to fill in the blank. To delete more than one character, repeatedly push or hold down the Del key.

Once you have deleted the mistake, you can type in the correct sequence. If you type a character within a line, the character will be inserted at the cursor location; any characters appearing to the right of the cursor will be automatically pushed one space farther to the right until you are done inserting characters, or until the entire line is filled, whichever occurs first.

When working on large documents, moving the cursor one character at at time with the arrow keys can be a slow and tedious process. To make editing easier, DR EDIX lets you move around the text in bigger increments by using the Home, End, PgUp, and PgDn keys from the numeric keypad. The PgUp and PgDn keys move the cursor 21 lines, or one page, up or down, respectively. The Home key automatically takes you to the first line of the document you're working on, while the End key will move you forward to the last line.

Additionally, function keys F3 and F4 will take you to the first and last lines of the page currently being displayed on your screen. F5 and F6 will move the cursor to the first and last characters in the current line.

Additional Editing Functions

Some of the more useful DR EDIX commands are presented in Table 6.2.

TABLE 6.2   Editing Command Summary

Command	Description
Alt A	Adds a blank line after the current line and moves the cursor to the beginning of that line.
Alt C	Copies the lines marked by the Alt K command to the line following the current line.
Alt D	Deletes the entire current line.
Alt E	Edit. Prompts you for the name of a new file to edit. Reads that file into DR EDIX. If another file is currently being edited, that file is erased before the new file is read.
Alt H	Presents the HELP screen.
Alt K	Marks the beginning or the end of a block of text. If a block is already specified, Alt K unmarks it.
Alt M	Moves the block marked by the Alt K command to the line following the current line.
Alt R	Read. Prompts you for the name of a file to read into DR EDIX. If another file is currently being edited, Alt R appends the new file to the end of that file.
Alt S	Search. Prompts you for a pattern and then searches for the next occurrence of that pattern.
Alt T	Translate. Prompts for a pattern to search for and a pattern to translate it to. When it finds the first match, it prompts for whether you wish to skip that occurrence, stop the translation, translate just that occurrence, or translate every occurrence in the document.
Alt U	Undo. Undoes the last Alt D deletion by inserting the last deleted line above the current line.
Alt X	Exits DR EDIX and returns to Concurrent.

Once you have finished working on a document and wish to file it away for later use, hold down the Alt key and press the W key (for WRITE). DR EDIX will prompt you for the filename where you wish to store the document. Typing in the filename and pressing <ENTER> will store the file away. To retrieve a file for further editing, hold down the Alt key and press E (for EDIT). When DR EDIX prompts you for the file, type in the name of the file you wish to work on and press <ENTER>. DR EDIX will read the file from disk and display it on your computer's screen for editing.

To exit DR EDIX, hold down the Alt key and press X. If you have not saved your work since last making changes to it, DR EDIX will remind you by presenting the following prompt in the status area:

OK to lose changes (y/n)?

If you wish to exit from DR EDIX without storing the newly created text, answer ''y'' (for yes) and press <ENTER>. If you wish to save the changes before exiting, type ''n'' and press <ENTER>. This will allow you to save the information in a file before exiting DR EDIX.

Buffers and Windows

When you read a file into DR EDIX for editing, the file is placed in memory in an area referred to as a buffer. DR EDIX has four buffers available for your use at one time, each of which can contain a separate file for editing. When you first start DR EDIX, buffer 1 is the current buffer. Any files you read in using the Alt R or Alt E command is read into buffer 1. To move to a different buffer area, hold down the Alt key and press the B key. A prompt will appear in the status area asking you to which buffer number or filename you wish to move. Type the number of the buffer, 1, 2, 3, or 4, that you wish to move to and press <ENTER> to move to that buffer. If you have previously read a file into a separate buffer, typing the name of that file followed by <ENTER> will move you to the proper buffer.

Having several buffers available allows you to work on more than one file at one time. However, sometimes you might wish to display the contents of two files on the screen at one time, perhaps for comparing the contents of the two files. DR EDIX allows you to do that by simultaneously displaying two buffers in separate regions on the screen referred to as windows.

Holding down the Alt key and pressing a ''2,'' the keyboard will split the screen horizontally and will display one window on the top half of the text area and one window on the bottom half. At any one time you can only type or perform actions in one window or the other. Holding down the Alt key and pressing the ''1'' or ''2'' key will switch you from one window to the other. To return to one full screen, hold down the Alt key and press the letter O.

To find out more about DR EDIX, including windows and buffers, refer to the documentation that is included with Concurrent PC DOS.

What DR EDIX Requires

During its execution, DR EDIX will use the following files.

DREDIX.CMD   Program file that is loaded into memory when you start
              DR EDIX
HELP.EDX   Contains the information for DR EDIX's HELP utility

In addition, the following files are required for using the DR EDIX tutorial program.

STUDENT.BAT   Concurrent PC DOS BATCH file that starts the
              tutorial program automatically
LSN.EDX   Contains the tutorial lessons
TEXT   Contains some sample text that will be used during the
              tutorial session.

DR EDIX requires approximately 120K of available memory in order to be used.

BACKUP AND RESTORE

Birth certificates, insurance policies, marriage licenses, wills, and other important documents are often tucked away at home in cupboards or drawers or filing cabinets. For an extra margin of safety, most people often keep a second copy of the most important documents stored away in a safety deposit box or some other secure place just in case the originals are somehow lost or misplaced. More often than not, the original will always be available and the copy may never be needed. However, should something happen to the original, having a backup copy available could prove to be a real lifesaver.

Similarly, having a backup copy of the information stored on disk can also prove to be a real lifesaver should something happen to the original copy. While both floppy disks and hard disks provide a convenient and reliable method of storing large amounts of information, accidents or malfunctions can and do occur. A floppy disk may be misplaced or could be damaged by a coffee spill. A hard disk could be damaged by a sharp jolt that causes the mechanics to go out of alignment. Or either one could be accidentally erased by mistyping a command.

While losing the only copy of your "Things To Do Today List" might be nothing more than an inconvenience, losing the only complete copy of your customer mailing list or all your IRS records may prove to be a much bigger problem. Since human beings are sometimes fallible creatures, having an up-to-date backup copy of your disks is always a good idea.

Making a backup copy of a floppy disk is a very simple exercise. Copying the entire contents of one disk to a second disk can be accomplished quickly and easily with Concurrent PC DOS using the COPY command or the File Manager. However, hard disks offer special problems. Because of the higher cost of a hard disk drive, maintaining a second hard disk for backup purposes is an expensive proposition (although depending on the quantity and importance of your data, it may actually be the best alternative).

Moving the information to floppy disks using the COPY command is an alternative. However, since the hard disk can hold more that 20 floppy disks' worth of data, organizing and copying the information on a regular basis and keeping track of all the disks can be a very tedious and time-consuming process.

The Better Way: Backup and Restore

Fortunately, a better way does exist. The backup and restore facility included in Concurrent PC DOS provides a convenient method for moving the information from your hard disk to floppy disks, and back again if necessary. The backup facility allows you to transfer data selectively. You can specify whether you wish to back up the contents of the entire hard disk or select just certain portions. You can choose specific files by name, grouping them by file name or file extensions.

If you keep files organized by subdirectories or by user numbers, you can specify which ones you want to back up. This ability allows you to back up just those data that you consider most important. Or if certain data change frequently, for instance, orders that are filled daily, having the capability to back up just that portion of your hard disk can save time.

Additionally, the Concurrent PC DOS backup facility can recognize which files have changed and which have not since the last backup was performed. Rather than taking the additional time to make yet another backup copy, only those files that have changed will be copied. Of course, at any time you can perform a backup of the entire disk again, if you wish.

The backup and restore facility is very easy to use. When the output floppy disk is full, it automatically prompts you to remove the full disk and insert another. To help keep track of the files, the backup facility tells you what to label each disk. Later, when it wants to restore a file from the floppy to the hard disk, it will prompt you to insert the proper disk, giving you the name of the disk that contains the correct file. To help you keep track of the process, a report is generated at the end of each backup or restore operation that specifies exactly what was done. To make the backup and restore procedure as easy as possible, both are accessible from the File Manager main menu.

How to Back Up Your Hard Disk

Both the backup and restore procedure use the file CONTROL.BR. This file contains specific information that tells the program how you want the backup or the restore operation to proceed. Included in the file is information specifying which files you want backed up, the type of printer you're using to generate the report, and whether to verify each file after it is copied to ensure accuracy. You can view or modify the contents of the file, and therefore specify different directions for the procedure, with any word processer or text editor, including DR EDIX. For safety's sake, make sure that you have a copy of the CONTROL.BR file before you make any changes to it, to ensure that a usable backup is always available. Full instructions for editing the CONTROL.BR file are included in the BACKREST.DOC file on a Concurrent PC DOS disk.

When you start the backup procedure, you will be prompted to insert floppy disks as required. If you are backing up a CP/M-formatted portion of your hard disk, you will be prompted to insert CP/M-formatted floppy disks; if you are backing up a PC DOS-formatted portion, you will be prompted to insert PC DOS-formatted floppy disks. Additionally, messages will be displayed on your computer's screen indicating the progress of the backup procedure. As each floppy disk is filled, you will be prompted to remove that disk and insert a new one. You will be prompted to label each disk with a specific name given by the program.

The first time the backup procedure is run, all the files, drives, subdirectories, or user numbers specified in the CONTROL.BR file will be copied to the backup floppy disks. To save time and floppy disks, every subsequent backup will only copy the files that have been modified since the previous backup was performed. Of course, at any time, a complete backup of all files can be performed again, at your discretion.

Restoring Files to Your Hard Disk

Since files are normally backed up for security, restoring files normally occurs only if data are lost. If data are lost because of accidental erasures, you may proceed with the restoral process without any cause for alarm. However, if the hard disk on your computer inexplicably loses data, contact a qualified service representative for troubleshooting and repair.

The restore procedure is very similar to the backup. Restore works from the information stored in the CONTROL.BR file. The restoration is interactive; you will be prompted when to install the various disks. All prompts will refer to the names given to the disks during the backup procedure. After the restoration is complete, a report will be generated indicating what files were restored.

For complete information on the backup and restore procedure, refer to the instructions included in the BACKREST.DOC file included on the Concurrent PC DOS distribution disks.

PRINTER MANAGER

One of the more useful features of Concurrent PC DOS is the Printer Manager. Printer Manager is a menu-driven program that allows you easily to print files created by other programs, such as word processors or spreadsheets. Besides being very easy to use, Printer Manager is a powerful program that can control up to five printers and can handle up to 254 files at one time. Printer Manager coordinates the routing of the various files to the printers as they are available.

Having the ability to specify multiple files to print at one time is a great convenience. Normal printer operations require you to specify only one file at a time for printing. If you have two files to print, you must wait for the first file to finish printing before you can specify the second. If you have several files to print, you need to stay near your computer in order to specify several separate print commands. Additionally, you wouldn't be able to use your computer for any other task while the files were being printed.

However, using Concurrent PC DOS with Printer Manager, you can specify multiple files at one time and still use your computer for other tasks during the print process. Printer Manager lets your computer print a number of files unattended, so that you can specify multiple files to be printed and leave for lunch. As soon as Printer Manager finishes one file, it automatically will go on to the next, without you having to be there to enter another print command. If you need more than one copy of a particular file or files, you can tell Printer Manager to make multiple copies, up to 254 copies, of any or all of the files you have specified to print.

You can also format files as you print them. This is especially useful for files that have not previously been formatted by a word processor. Printer Manager allows you to control the number of lines printed per page and the margins to be used.

Printer Manager works transparently and does not take up one of Concurrent PC DOS's four windows. To use Printer Manager, you start it in one of Concurrent's four windows, either from the main menu or by typing in a command from the command line prompt. Once you start printing files you can leave Printer Manager and use that window for running another program. Printer Manager will continue to send the contents of all the files you specified to the available printer. At any time you can view the status of Printer Manager, specify additional files to be printed, or remove files from the list of files that remain to be printed.

With its powerful features and ability to control the print process automatically, Printer Manager is an ideal solution to the problem of several people sharing the computer. Rather than having two or three people trying to coordinate the use of one or more printers, Printer Manager turns that responsibility over to the computer so that it can take care of the various requests for printer resources. Whenever you want to print a file, you simply give the filename to Printer Manager. When the printer becomes available, Printer Manager will automatically route the contents of the file to it, saving you from the inconvenience of waiting around for a printer to free up.

Starting the Printer Manager

To start Printer Manager on a hard-disk-based computer that has Concurrent installed, press function key F6 from the Concurrent startup menu. The Concurrent Printer Manager main menu displayed in Figure 6.5 will appear on your screen.

To start the Printer Manager on a two-floppy-disk-based computer, copy the files HDMENU.DAT, PRINTMGR.CMD, SPL.CMD, and DSP.CMD to a CP/M-formatted disk. This disk will serve as your Printer Manager working disk. After you have started Concurrent, exit from the Concurrent startup menu to the command line prompt by pressing the Esc key and place your working disk in the system drive. From the command line prompt, type in the command

A>RUNMENU HDMENU.DAT PRINTMGR<ENTER>

The Concurrent Printer Manager menu displayed in Figure 6.5 will appear on your screen. Printer Manager will use the working disk to store information

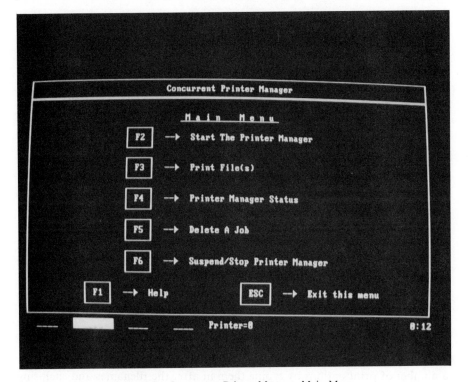

Figure 6.5 Concurrent Printer Manager Main Menu

while it is running. Leave the working disk in the system drive until you are finished using Printer Manager.

Before Printer Manager can start printing files, you must specify which printers are available for use. Concurrent allows up to five printers to be attached to your computer. Printers 0, 1, and 2 are defined as parallel printers. Printers 3 and 4 are serial printers. Refer to the documentation supplied by the manufacturer of your computer and printer to determine which type of printer you are using.

To specify one or more printers for use by Printer Manager, select the START THE PRINTER MANAGER option from the Printer Manager main menu by pressing function key F2. From there, select the correct printer or printers by pressing the appropriate function key. When you select a printer, Printer Manager will display a message indicating whether or not it was successful in connecting to that printer.

Now That You've Started

Once you have started the Printer Manager and have specified the printer or printers to be used during your session, return to the Printer Manager main menu by pressing the Esc key. As you use Printer Manager you will be moving through a series of menus in order to perform certain actions. All actions you can take during the session will be started from the main menu. Remember that with Concurrent you can move back to a previous menu at any time by pressing the Esc key.

Throughout the Printer Manager menu system you will be presented with the option to select HELP by pressing function key F1. Selecting HELP will present you with more information pertaining to the current menu that you happen to be in. If, at any time, you are not sure of the correct way to proceed, HELP can explain the available options and guide you along the best path. After you finish using HELP, you will be returned to the same place where you left off.

To specify which files you wish to print, select the "PRINT FILE(S)" option from the main menu by pressing function key F3, followed by F2, "SPECIFY FILE(S) TO PRINT," from the next menu. The following message will appear on the bottom of the screen and the flashing cursor will appear next to it:

>PRINTMGR PRINT __

Enter the complete name of the file that you wish to print. You can specify a number of print options by typing them in after the filenames and enclosing the options in square brackets. The options selected will be applied to each of the files that have been listed. A list of the available options is displayed in Table 6.3. You can enter as many filenames and options as will fit on the line. Separate multiple filenames with a space and multiple options with a comma.

TABLE 6.3   Printer Manager Menu Options

Command	Description
COPIES = n	Print n copies of the file specified; N can be from 1 to 254; if not specified, Printer Manager will print one copy
FORMAT	When specified, prints 55 lines per page; assumes standard page size of 66 lines
FORMSIZE = n	Sets page size for n lines; if not specified, assumes standard page size of 66 lines
MARGIN = n	Set a left margin of n spaces; if not specified, sets left margin for eight spaces
NOFEED	When specified, does not send form feed to printer between files; if not specified, form feed sent to printer between files
NUMBER	Same as FORMAT, but in addition, numbers each page
PAGESIZE = n	Prints n lines per page
PRINTER = n	Send output to printer n; if not specified, sends output to current printer
TABS = n	Sets tab stop to every n columns; if not specified, sets tab stop to every eight columns

If no options are specified, one copy of each file will be printed exactly as they appear in the file, except that the left margin will be set at eight spaces and tabs will be set to every eight columns. The output will be continuous (no top or bottom margin will appear on each page) unless form feeds are included in the file.

FORMAT and NUMBER are normally used for standard-size printer paper 11 inches long and standard printers that print six lines per inch. If nonstandard paper is used or your printer prints more or less than six lines per inch, use the FORMSIZE and PAGESIZE options to reflect the printer's settings.

The following example demonstrates what would be entered in order to print three copies of files LETTER.TXT and MEMO.JR with 55 lines per page, with each page numbered and printed on a standard-size printer page by a standard printer.

>PRINTMGR PRINT LETTER.TXT MEMO.JR [COPIES = 3,NUMBER]

Once you have specified the appropriate files and options, the print process will start and you will be prompted to hit any key to return to the PRINT FILES menu. Once back at the PRINT FILES menu, you can specify additional files to be added to the print list by repeating the procedure outlined above, or you can return to the Printer Manager main menu by pressing the Esc key.

Printer Manager Status

At any time you can determine the current status of Printer Manager. From the Printer Manager main menu select PRINTER MANAGER STATUS by pressing function key F4. A sample status screen is displayed in Figure 6.6.

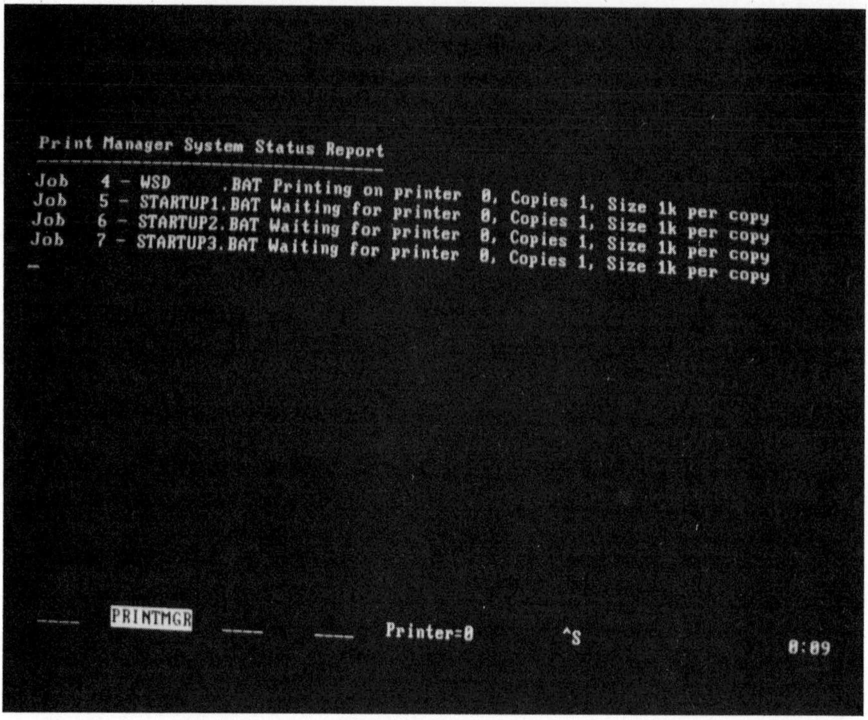

```
Print Manager System Status Report
------------------------------------------------
Job    4 - WSD      .BAT Printing on printer   0, Copies 1, Size 1k per copy
Job    5 - STARTUP1.BAT Waiting for printer    0, Copies 1, Size 1k per copy
Job    6 - STARTUP2.BAT Waiting for printer    0, Copies 1, Size 1k per copy
Job    7 - STARTUP3.BAT Waiting for printer    0, Copies 1, Size 1k per copy
-


     PRINTMGR     ----       ----      Printer=0          ^S                    0:09
```

Figure 6.6   Printer Manager Status Display

You will notice that each file to be printed is assigned a job number by the Printer Manager. The job number is important and will be discussed later when dealing with deleting files from the Printer Manager. The Printer Manager status displays the files currently active, whether the files are being printed or are waiting for a printer to become available, the printer number that the file is assigned to, how many copies remain to be printed for each file, the size of each file in kilobytes, and the job number assigned to each file. From the status display, return to the Printer Manager main menu by pressing any key.

Deleting a File from Printer Manager

When you specify a file to be printed from the Printer Manager, that file is added to the list reported by the Printer Manager status display talked about in the preceding section. If, after adding a file to the Printer Manager, you should change your mind and wish to remove the file from the list, you can accomplish that through the DELETE A JOB option from the Printer Manager main menu. To select DELETE A JOB, press function key F5 from the main menu. The DELETE A JOB menu will appear on your computer's display. To proceed, press function key F2, "SPECIFY JOB TO DELETE." The flashing cursor will appear on the bottom of the screen next to the following prompt:

>PRINTMGR DELETE __

Type in the number of the job you wish to delete and press <ENTER>. You can determine the job number of the file you wish to delete through the Printer Manager status discussed in the preceeding section. After you specify the job number to be deleted, a message will be displayed indicating whether the deletion was successful, and you will be prompted to press any key in order to return to the DELETE A JOB menu. From there, you can either specify another job to be deleted or you can return to the Printer Manager main menu by pressing the Esc key.

Exiting Printer Manager

After you have finished adding or deleting files to be printed, you can exit Printer Manager by pressing the Esc key from the Printer Manager main menu. This will return you to the Concurrent PC DOS startup menu. From there you can proceed with any other program or activity you wish to run. Printer Manager will continue to run without any further intervention until all the files specified have been printed.

At any time you can return to Printer Manager to add files to the list to be printed, to delete files from the list, or to view the status of the Printer Manager. To return to the Printer Manager, press function key F6 from the Concurrent startup menu. If you left the Printer Manager running, you do not have to start it again by selecting function key F2 from the Printer Manager main menu. You can proceed directly to the PRINT FILE(S), PRINTER MANAGER STATUS, or the DELETE A JOB selection.

If you wish to halt execution of the Printer Manager, you can do so by selecting function key F6, "SUSPEND/STOP PRINTER MANAGER," from the Printer Manager main menu. If you select this option, you will be presented with another menu, displaying the choices F2, "SUSPEND THE PRINTER MANAGER," and F3, "STOP THE PRINTER MANAGER."

The choice "SUSPEND THE PRINTER MANAGER" will halt any output to the printer and will save the current status of the Printer Manager. A message indicating that the Printer Manager has been suspended will appear on the screen and you will be prompted to press any key in order to return to the suspend/stop Printer Manager menu. Pressing Esc will return you to the Printer Manager main menu. From there you can either exit the Printer Manager by pressing Esc, returning to the Concurrent PC DOS main menu, or you can restart the Printer Manager.

To restart the Printer Manager you will have to select the "START THE

PRINTER MANAGER'' option and specify again which printers are available for the Printer Manager to use. When you restart the Printer Manager, the print process will resume at the point where you suspended the Printer Manager. All print jobs will be resumed where they were left off.

Selecting F3, "STOP THE PRINTER MANAGER," will also stop the print process and display a message indicating that the Printer Manager was stopped. You will be prompted to press any key to return to the suspend/stop Printer Manager menu. However, the list of files waiting to be printed will be deleted when you choose the "STOP THE PRINT MANAGER" option. If you wish to print any files, you must first start the Printer Manager and select the printers to be used. You must then specify any files you wish to print and any appropriate options. For more information on starting the Printer Manager, refer to the section above entitled "Now That You've Started."

What Printer Manager Requires

During its execution, the Printer Manager will use the following files.

PRINTMGR.CMD	Program file that is loaded into memory as Printer Manager is executed

SPL.CMD	Program file used during the execution of Printer Manager

DSP.CMD	Program file used during the execution of Printer Manager

MENU.DAT	Contains the menu system used by Concurrent PC DOS and the File Manager on a hard-disk-based computer

If you are using Concurrent on a two-floppy-disk-based computer, you will not use MENU.DAT. Instead, you will use the HDMENU.DAT file as outlined in the section "Starting the Printer Manager."

Printer Manager requires 128K of available memory in order to be used.

7

CONCURRENT CASE STUDIES

Describing the features and facilities of concurrency is one way to approach the subject. Depicting it in action is another. In the section that follows, we look at a variety of work environments that have significantly benefited from the power of concurrency. Attorneys, programmers, real estate agents, doctors, brokers, and business managers are dealt with here. However, you can see that a common thread runs through all these occupations: the need to deal with large amounts of information and manipulate that information in complex ways. This would ordinarily tie up a computer and prevent other tasks from being able to be performed. As we will see, this no longer has to be the case.

It is handy to have programs waiting on other "screens" at your beck and call—without having to load and unload them all the time. It is also helpful to have one program feed data as input into another. It is quite useful to be able to print a mailing list, customer lists, or program list without having to take a mandatory coffee break each time. For these reasons and many others, concurrent processing is being considered essential to those who experience a heavy demand placed on their talents and professional resources.

As we have discussed previously in this book, Concurrent offers the opportunity to work in a totally integrated environment while simultaneously performing more than one task. As more independent software vendors produce programs that make full use of this multiuser, multitasking operation system, there will become a greater variety of powerful software systems designed for specific occupations. These specific programs are often referred to as "vertical market" applications.

At the time of publication of this book there is a shortage of vertical market applications that are designed to take full advantage of a multiuser, multitasking operating system. For this reason we will present suggested system configurations that can fulfill the needs of specific occupations in a simple, ergonomic manner.

CASE STUDY: THE CORPORATE MANAGERIAL OFFICE

Accounting
Administration
Marketing
Personnel
Sales

Administrative offices within large organizations very often perform similar tasks and thus have similar information-processing needs. Organizing informational input is one of the organization's major functions, and creating and disseminating new informational output is another. Between these two operations are the processes of analysis, deliberation, and judgment. The more we can streamline any one of these operations or processes, the more we can enhance the overall operational throughput. In other words, the more efficient we become, the more we can accomplish.

Sorting out and logging in the new information is done by entering this information into an on-line filing system to facilitate quick retrieval and easy updating. Creating and disseminating information is done with a word-processing system in conjunction with a graphing program to provide visual impact along with the words.

The analysis phase is aided by a variety of programs that relate to the particular field: project scheduling and monitoring, financial spreadsheets, electronic communications, and technical computation. In addition to these operations there are various housekeeping chores that are convenient to have on a computer: a name and address filer, an appointment calendar, and an automatic phone dialer, among others.

The computer has a great deal of capacity to handle each of these operations individually. Concurrency brings increased capacity to handle each of these operations by letting them work collectively. Since you can have four of these programs operating at any one time, this can greatly improve the work flow.

Consider the marketing manager who is creating a presentation for a new product with a word processor loaded on one window and a graph generating program loaded on another. The manager is able to write the presentation, break away to the graph program to create visuals as an idea occurs, and then return to writing at the press of a key. On the third window the name and address filer is searching for all the entries with a certain ZIP code to build a mailing list without interrupting the other operations. The manager will switch screens periodically to see if the search has been completed and if so, start another one.

On the fourth window is loaded a calculator program that allows figures to be checked before they are put into the presentation. The manager is able to work very efficiently by having all the tools required for these tasks readily available. Following is an example of how these activities look.

Task	Description	Location
1	Writing presentation	Screen 1
2	Creating graphs	Screen 2
3	Building mailing list	Screen 3
4	Checking calculations	Screen 4

When the presentation is finished, screen 1 can have the presentation printed on the letter-quality printer, while screen 2 has the graphs printed on the plotter and screens 3 and 4 are used for other purposes.

Let us say that our second manager works in the personnel department and has to mail a letter to every employee whose W-2 form lists over six exemptions. Furthermore, the letter must include calculations that tell what the new estimated monthly payroll deduction will be for each employee so identified.

Here is how the computer is set up under Concurrent. On the first window, the data base program that contains all current W-2 information is used to search for those employees who are claiming seven or more exemptions. On window 2 a spreadsheet program is loaded that uses an algorithm within it that generates the numbers needed for the form letter when the input from the employee's W-2 form is entered. On window 3 a mailing list program is running that has the form letter loaded and waiting for the information.

When the data base search locates an appropriate employee, the information is extracted from the W-2; the manager then switches windows to the spreadsheet and enters it. The spreadsheet generates the new deduction figure for that employee. That figure is then taken to window 3, where an appropriate copy of the form letter is sent to that employee with the deduction entered in the space provided. That letter is then printed with its unique information, and the manager goes back to the data base, which has continued searching while the other tasks were being performed. When the manager comes back to the mailing list program, a fresh copy of the form letter will be waiting for new input.

In addition, on window 4, a modem has been installed that provides access to the company's mainframe computer. That's where the previous year's withholding tax information is stored. Occasionally, the manager checks back to compare current figures with last year's data. This activity can be accomplished merely by pressing a few keys and without disturbing the processes that are ongoing.

These are some of the activities that managers can perform more effectively using the Concurrent operating system. Once the system is installed on a computer, it is easy for a manager to find a variety of ways to use Concurrent to increase efficiency.

CASE STUDY: THE REAL ESTATE OFFICE

Real Estate Office
Property Management
Loan Office
Mortgage Brokers
Banks

The real estate office is a complex business environment requiring that a variety of functions be performed. There are extensive calculations to be performed to qualify potential home buyers, to determine the terms of private financing, and to calculate closing statements with allocations and prorations. There are several data bases to be managed: properties for sale, client lists, properties going through escrow, rental units being managed, and mortgages being granted by local lenders with their rates, types, and terms.

Not all offices do all things, but we will discuss a small office and a full service office to illustrate how the Concurrent processing environment can bring widespread efficiency to a complex business environment no matter what its size. Specialized firms that only do property management or mortgages, for instance, would also benefit from the Concurrent processing environment, as would loan departments in banks and savings and loans, and therefore these are also mentioned here.

Single-User Computer: Small Office Model

We begin with the smaller office with a staff of three to five people. For this office to function at all, each person has to be capable of doing a variety of jobs. Since efficiency is crucial, this office probably already has a personal computer or at least a dial-up connection to a computer downtown that is shared by many similar offices.

The problem is, of course, that there is more work to be done than time to do it and people must work long hours. If you want to get on the computer, you have to come in early or stay late. Weekends are already committed to open houses. Home lives are disrupted. Work falls behind. Besides the calculations and listings, there is a mountain of correspondence for the word processor and the office's own accounting has to be updated. What's to be done?

In the single-user Concurrent system, four tasks can be operating at one time on the computer. Today we have a property management program running on window 1, and rent payments are being credited to each unit and each property. One of the checks bounced, it is noted, for unit 12 in the building at 756 Pebble. We then switch to window 2, where we have a word-processing program running. We write a short but firm dunning letter to the occupant concerning the bad check, send the letter to the printer, and switch back to posting the rents.

On window 3 we are running a data base program that contains a price comparison file—prices and brief descriptions of all houses in the community that have sold in the last six months. A time ago we started sorting for all homes between $125,000 and $150,000 with four bedrooms, ranch-style design, a two-car garage, and a fireplace. We now switch to window 3 and see that there are 15 listings. We send this batch of listings to the printer, where our dunning letter has finished printing, so we can take the list to Mr. & Mrs. Logan. This list will be a good reference when we discuss what price to ask for their house when it goes on the market next week.

We begin another such search for the Gutierrez property, with two bedrooms, a carport, large lot, and all appliances included. We will check back in a few minutes to see what the results are. Back to window 1 and the rent posting that is almost finished. When we have finished the posting and calculating the extra charges, we can send these data to the disk that is logged in to window 4, where we have an accounts receivable program running. When we go to that program in window 4 to post the income from the management fees on the properties, the figures will be there waiting for us. In the meantime we are making a list of lease renewal dates for the next three months and merging the names and addresses with our form letter for lease renewal.

Let's review what we've done. The list below shows what processes were being done on each of the four windows on our computer using the Concurrent system.

Window	Task	Output
1	Property management	Disk file
2	Word processor	Letter printed
3	Data base search	List printed
4	Accounts receivable	Disk file

Multiuser Computer: Large Office Model

While the small office had many people sharing a single machine, one at a time, this model has three people sharing a single machine at the same time. Because Concurrent PC DOS can accommodate two terminals connected to serial ports of the host computer, it makes possible a powerful multiuser configuration. Each of the satellite terminals can run only one application, however, but the host computer can run up to four at a time. This means that tasks not needing interactivity should run on the terminals rather than the host computer, if possible.

For instance, in this scenario, one terminal is dedicated to word processing. An agent is writing advertising copy for the weekend ad. On another terminal, an agent is running a mortgage payment program and trying to find suitable loan terms and payment schedules for a customer with marginal financial resources. Meanwhile on the host computer, the office business manager is running an accounts receivable program in window 1, a payroll/commission program in window 2, and the general ledger loaded on window 3.

Window 4 is kept available for running emergency tasks for others in the office on a moment's notice. This way the business manager doesn't have to close a file and unload a program before running their emergency program. There's a terminal waiting for them. The manager will tolerate only brief interruption, however. If the task will take longer than a few minutes, arrangements will be made to use one of the terminals.

As the manager switches from window to window, calculating and producing commission checks on one, compiling agent chargebacks on another and reconciling transactions with the general ledger, she reflects on how cumbersome this process was when she could not operate interactively. Concurrency has allowed her to use the same time over and over to get several tasks done instead of just one at a time. She can't imagine working without it anymore.

CASE STUDY: THE MEDICAL OR THERAPEUTIC PRACTICE

Physicians

Dentists

Psychologists

Psychiatrists

Therapists

Counselors

Chiropractors

Practitioners of the healing arts and sciences find their professions becoming more complex every day. Not only must they keep abreast of ever-expanding literature in their field, but must also cope with the growing complexity of running an office. Insurance requirements, for example, have become so complex that many practices have put the burden back onto the patient. This then created the problem of generating two types of billing, since not all accounts could be placed back on the patient.

The requirements of state and federal government reporting have grown; in a large practice this can be a full-time job in itself without computer aid.

The advent of the computer made a great difference to a practice, but it was not the total solution to office efficiency.

Before Concurrent

Since the microcomputer could handle only one thing at a time, the medical office still had a number of people doing clerical tasks that the computer could have eliminated. While it was being used for keeping the appointment schedule, it could not be used for billing. Printing bills kept anyone from using it for data look-up in patient master files. Using it for data look-up meant that no one could then log in a new appointment.

Each time it was used for one dedicated purpose, others had to make notes and do their work later or make estimates off the top of their heads with the attendant margin of error. Anything not entered into the system when it was generated risks being entered incorrectly or not at all. Answers given out that did not have the benefit of an accurate look-up could be embarrassing at a later time or require another phone call or letter of clarification. By scheduling access to the computer, some of these problems could be solved. Staggered lunchtimes, evening work, and weekend work—all of these help cover for the inadequacies of the single-user system.

After Concurrent

Since Concurrent is not only multitasking but also has multiuser capability as well, it is well suited for the medical office. When two terminals can be connected to the host computer, one can be placed by the reception desk and dedicated to logging in appointments. Another can be dedicated to insurance form preparation. Since these terminals can handle only a single task, they are placed strategically so that they can be used for those tasks that need to be done throughout the day.

The host computer is located in the office manager's office. Even though each of the terminals is being used, under Concurrent the host computer still has the ability to handle four tasks. [You recall that the area that each task (program) runs in is called a window.] This means that window 1 can be running the program that prints the patient monthly statements, while in window 2 the office manager is cross-posting charges for consulting physicians. Window 3 has the master patient data base loaded and a sort is being run on patients who have used or are using a relatively new medication on which the FDA has just issued a warning.

When the list of patients is complete, the manager will go to window 4 and use the word-processing program to write and then have printed a cautionary letter to those patients. To summarize, we can see that the system is being efficiently used. Three people are working on it doing up to six things at one time.

Here's how it looks:

Task	Description	Location
1	Appointments	Terminal A
2	Insurance forms	Terminal B
3	Billing	Window 1
4	Posting	Window 2
5	Data base search	Window 3
6	Word processor	Window 4

Remember that tasks 1 and 2 will stay the same all day. That's the way this system has been configured. They could do other things, however, but only one thing at a time. The host computer, however, with its four windows, can be running four programs at a time while the operator moves back and forth among them monitoring their output. Up to four printers can be in the system, although two—one letter quality for correspondence, one dot matrix for statements and reports—are usually enough.

Many other configurations are, of course, possible. Let's look at another. Again, we will have a terminal dedicated to appointments, since whoever is working the front counter will be interrupted often. That would not be a good place to put the host computer. The second terminal is used this time for transcription of doctor's tapes of examination data. That means a word processor and printing capability. When the printed transcripts are completed, they are inserted into the patient's file. A copy goes back to the doctor, who reviews it and highlights salient features that are later to be added to the patient master file.

The host computer, in this case, is placed in a central area where many people have access to it. Window 1 contains a schedule program, not of patients this time but of the doctor's outside speaking engagements, on call schedule, and yes, even the golf game next Wednesday. This scheduler also shows which patients are scheduled into the hospital, when and who has been referred to another practitioner, and when that referral took place.

Window 2 is busy building a year-to-date report of procedure frequencies with dollar totals. In window 3, a recall list is being compiled to enable the staff to send out reminders to those who are due for a checkup. Window 4 is currently in use by the accountant to review the aged account section of the receivables list. When this list is prepared, it will be available to the word processor terminal and for inserting into dunning letters that are typed and sent to all those whose accounts are more than 90 days overdue (the table on page 81 shows how it looks).

Tasks that used to have to compete for the computer or were done without a computer are now being done on the system concurrently, which saves

Task	Description	Location
1	Appointments	Terminal A
2	Word processing	Terminal B
3	Scheduler	Window 1
4	Data base search	Window 2
5	Data base search	Window 3
6	Accounts receivable	Window 4

time, effort, hardware, and aggravation. The introduction of concurrent micro-computers will have as great an impact on the operation of a medical office as the introduction of the microcomputer itself has had.

CASE STUDY: THE MICROCOMPUTER PROGRAMMER

The working environment of a programmer is quite different from that of a business person or professional. Development of software on micro-computers using a compiled language often creates long periods of waiting for a compile before being able to continue with the debugging of code. It doesn't matter what language you are using. Whether it be C, Pascal, or CBASIC, the process remains the same. Let's discuss the way in which a program is created to better understand how a person might use Concurrent to achieve a better working situation.

First you design a solution to your problem; then you implement that solution by writing the source code that will be compiled into intermediate code and linked with the libraries of defined functions required by the specific high-level language you are using. This process creates the machine-level in-structions that become your "executable" program.

Then you must "debug" the code and start again at the beginning of the process by making modifications to your original source code, recompile, relink, and retest. This process continues time after time until the program accomplishes what it was designed to accomplish. It is a very rare instance when a program is created correctly in one try. We do not need to delve too deeply into pro-gram design to see the advantages of the Concurrent multiprocessing environ-ment. In the Concurrent environment, the programmer can be accomplishing more than one of these tasks at a time.

First let's visualize program design in a single-tasking environment (Figure 7.1). One of the advantages of the multitasking environment is the ability to develop several programs at the same time without tying up all of the micro-computer resources. A programmer working in the Concurrent environment can work on several programs at one time. Additionally, more information is

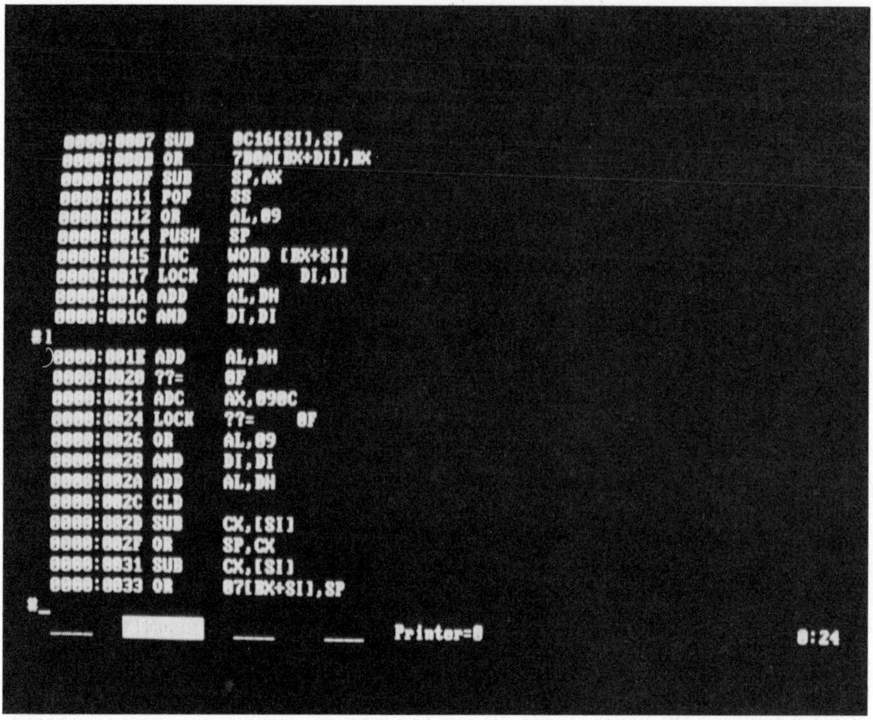

```
0000:0007 SUB     0C16[SI],SP
0000:000D OR      7D0A[BX+DI],BX
0000:000F SUB     SP,AX
0000:0011 POP     SS
0000:0012 OR      AL,09
0000:0014 PUSH    SP
0000:0015 INC     WORD [BX+SI]
0000:0017 LOCK    AND     DI,DI
0000:001A ADD     AL,DH
0000:001C AND     DI,DI
#1
)0000:001E ADD    AL,DH
0000:0020 ??=     0F
0000:0021 ADC     AX,090C
0000:0024 LOCK    ??=     0F
0000:0026 OR      AL,09
0000:0028 AND     DI,DI
0000:002A ADD     AL,DH
0000:002C CLD
0000:002D SUB     CX,[SI]
0000:002F OR      SP,CX
0000:0031 SUB     CX,[SI]
0000:0033 OR      07[BX+SI],SP
#_
_____    _____   _____    _____   Printer=0                    0:24
```

Figure 7.1   Programming in a Single-Tasking Environment

available through the use of windows. By the creation of windows a programmer can monitor the background processes, those that are not actually being worked on at that moment, to determine when they are completed.

A Sample Programming Session

As Figure 7.2 shows, several processes can be operating at the same time during multitasking programming. One thing that must be considered at this point is the SUSPEND mode, which controls the type of activity that may occur in the background processes. Because Digital Research languages are "well behaved," they do not write directly to the screen and may operate as background processes. Most other compilers are also well behaved, although many word processors and most games are not. Check with the manufacturer of a program to determine if it directly accesses the video screen.

Window 1: In this window you are reediting program 1's source code with a word processor. You have already completed the first compile of program 1 and discovered that there were some mistakes.

Window 2: In this window you are using a debugger, such as SID86 to

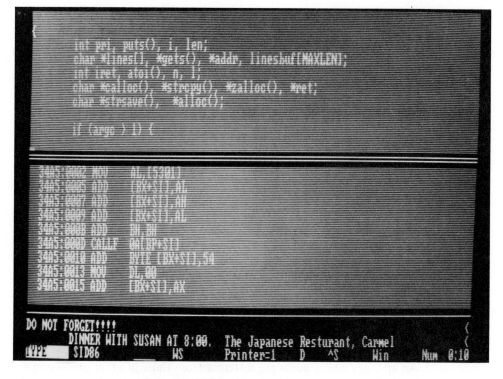

Figure 7.2 Multitasking Programming

examine the code of program 1 that you have produced in the compile. In this way you may make modifications in window 1 while actually seeing this code.

Window 3: This window is operating as a background process compiling another program that you are developing.

Window 4: This window is maintaining clock and schedule functions to keep track of your meetings and other commitments while you are working.

Now we will present the .BAT files that were used to create the sample screen above. You may type these onto your computer as is, or modify them in any way that you choose.

Now let's review some of the advantages for a microcomputer programmer working in the Concurrent environment.

One of the most important advantages of a multitasking operating system is that it increases the efficiency of both the programmer and the microcomputer. This is accomplished in two ways: first, the programmer spends much less time waiting for processing to complete and much more time actually coding; and second, when text editing in a single-tasking operating system, the computer spends most of its time waiting for input, whereas in a multitasking system the computer continues with the background tasks while the operator is text editing.

The increase in computer efficiency is not limited to the times when performing text editing functions. At any moment the processor is not being used by a program, it is directed to another task. A second major advantage to working in the Concurrent environment is that it speeds the development of a program. This can help to get it to market earlier and thus increase the profitability of the program.

Third, the programmer can increase his or her knowledge and abilities through techniques such as the examination of source code and the actual executable code at the same time. This improves the ability to write machine code by the simultaneous examination of the high-level code. The line-by-line comparison of the machine code examined by different high-level compilers is quite helpful.

In summary, the multitasking environment of Concurrent PC-DOS frees the programmer from many of the limitations of microcomputer program design. This freedom allows the programmer to increase both knowledge and productivity.

CASE STUDY: THE ATTORNEY

An attorney whose needs are different from those of other professionals can also profit tremendously from the capabilities provided by Concurrent PC-DOS. The attorney is frequently a specialist in one aspect of law and tends to perform the same type of service repetitively within a short period of time. Some of the tools that an attorney might require range from a word-processing program to specialized software designed to handle resource scheduling, billing, and general reference information.

In addition, there are on-line data bases that bring the power of information to the office of an isolated attorney. Concurrent facilitates the use of many types of programs interchangably without the inconvenience of having to change software and wait while it reloads in order to gain access to the information required.

Another feature of Concurrent that is of particular significance to the attorney is that it is multiuser and thus supports more than one terminal. Usually, an attorney is sharing an office with at least one other attorney and frequently shares secretarial services. A Concurrent system can service up to three workstations at a fraction of the cost of other systems, and thus place all shared information into the hands of each user. In the sample situation, we will deal with a single attorney who has equipped his secretary with an additional terminal.

First let's examine where this attorney locates and connects the equipment. The computer is located in the attorney's private office. This makes it the main workstation or host with four windows. The secretary has only one virtual console available on the separate terminal.

The attorney likes to keep the scheduling software always accessible in order to make notes when talking to someone and because entering each conversation allows the software to determine the client's charges automatically. The built-in clock in his computer is accessed by this software many times each second, keeping very accurate records. There are many types of legal software available for this system. For more information on specific packages, consult your computer salesperson.

The attorney uses another window for communicating with any of a number of electronic data bases. This attorney subscribes to four—CompuServe, DIALOG, LEXIS, and WESTLAW—and uses each for different purposes. This morning DIALOG is being used to perform a trademark search. This service that used to have to be performed out of the office, causing a wait of several days for an answer, can now be determined in a matter of minutes. Once the search is completed the information is inserted into a complaint that is being prepared on another console. DR TALK is used to communicate with these data bases and is also used as a phone directory that places phone calls automatically. When the information is located on DIALOG, it is displayed in a window at the bottom of the screen so that it may be transferred to the word processor as it is being viewed.

In a third window the word processor is installed for working on the outline of the complaint. When the complaint is finished the secretary will finalize it by making certain that it contains all the information that is desired in each document that is sent out. The secretary will do this work from the terminal since it shares the hard disk on the computer and may be used to access any files that are not protected with a secret password.

In the fourth window the attorney searches the data base that has been compiled of local cases to see which judge has ruled most often in a favorable manner on a similar case. The information in this data base is entered each day by the secretary at the terminal. This is critical information to the attorney, as it will be used in an attempt to have the client's case tried under the most favorable conditions.

The attorney is not always using the computer, but the programs that are used are always loaded and the information is always available. The secretary uses the separate terminal for many different jobs, loading the software for each job as it is required. This morning the secretary is entering information into the local data base at the same time that the attorney is searching through it. This can be done because they are using a multiuser data base system.

Concurrency is very important in this situation, because it means that all the power of the computer is available at the touch of a key. The attorney can switch between windows immediately, making use of the various software packages easy rather than the chore it was under the single-user, single-tasking operating system that was used previously. Additionally, the secretary now has access to all the host software without having to have another computer.

CASE STUDY: THE FINANCIAL ANALYST

The basic types of software currently available for financial investing permit the analyst to integrate the work space and to maintain a constant watch on price fluctuations. In the past the analyst could receive data from the daily tickers, but it had to be recorded manually. With many of the software packages available today, the data can be captured on disk to be analyzed by another piece of software.

There are also graphing packages that can be used to make graphs of the data that have been collected. Much of this has only become available to many analysts since personal computers have achieved their current level of popularity. With Concurrent PC DOS the analyst can integrate many of these functions in more ways than ever before possible.

Figure 7.3 shows a comparison of profit to price over a period of time and is of the type that can be generated by some software packages available in most local computer stores. This particular graph was created with DR GRAPH, another Digital Research product.

The types of packages designed specifically for the analyst fall into two major categories: analysis and management. Some of the most sophisticated

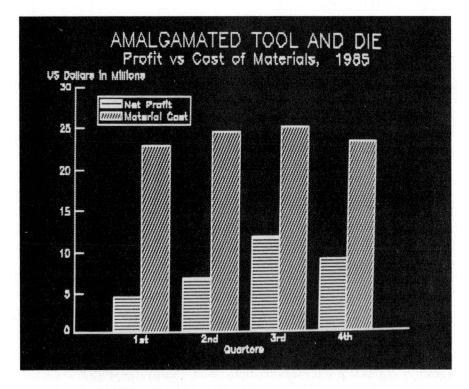

Figure 7.3 Typical Graph Showing Profit as Compared to Price across Time

pieces of software will automatically access a data base by telephone, collect information on the chosen stocks, perform statistical analysis of the information, and even warn of changes in predetermined indicators of potential price fluctuations.

There are also management programs that will allow the analyst to make transactions while creating a history of them. With some of the more sophisticated systems, it becomes very important for the user to be aware of the assumptions of the person who designed the software in order to be fully aware of the messages that are given.

In this sample session we will integrate some of the more useful functions of the software currently being used by many analysts and suggest a possible configuration for the investor.

The analyst is interested in always displaying the ticker during market hours and has the software to do that. With Concurrent the information that the software generates can be displayed in a window at the bottom of the screen, where it can be monitored while the computer is used to perform other duties. On the top portion of the screen the analyst switches from process to process as the required tasks change. The printer is often working as a background task printing a graph or report.

In this particular example the analyst is using three pieces of software on the top half of the screen while the bottom section is reserved for display of the ticker. When using Concurrent you may always bring the screen that you are using into the foreground of the whole screen by pressing the Ctrl and Del keys simultaneously.

8

THE MECHANICS OF CONCURRENT

After you ask "What can Concurrent do?" you may want to ask "What can't it do?" To understand the nature of the operating system at its deepest levels is not our goal here. We do, however, want to go into some of the mechanics that create the visible portion of the system—the "window-switching" feature and some of its implications.

As we mentioned earlier, in terms of concurrent processing, programs can be "well behaved" or "poorly behaved." Well-behaved programs are like polite salespersons who check with the secretary before dropping in on a client. A poorly behaved program would ignore the secretary and any other rules as well. This program breaks in on someone without warning. After hours, he probably crashes parties as well. Anyway, when this poorly behaved program "drops in," he causes problems.

How does this behavior problem manifest itself in our work on the computer? In general, it means that a program can be doing things that we don't want it to do or won't do things that we do want it to, because it is operating out of its normal environment. The most dramatic example of this in our area of concern is what is called "writing directly to the screen." In order to have Concurrent share the physical screen—the glass tube you can touch—among the four "windows" or programs that can be running simultaneously, there needs to be some traffic control.

In other words, when a program is running in a window that is not being viewed on the physical screen, it sends the screen information to a "buffer" or holding area until it can go to the screen. When you "switch-in" that window, that screen information is available instantaneously for viewing. Since we have up to four windows doing this, that means we have up to four screen buffers loaded at any given time. Each one will send information to the actual screen that you are viewing when it is called on and not before (or after for that matter). That's the way its supposed to be. Programs that are designed to run in this environment obey the rules and everything is fine.

But when a program breaks the rules of the new environment (we can't blame it; it didn't know it would be there), it causes a problem. How does this look to the viewer? Let's say that you are trying to compute a monthly sales report on your spreadsheet program in window 1. You initiate a lengthy calculation and while the computer is pondering that, you switch to window 2 to write a letter to your northern regional office.

As you write the letter, the spreadsheet program begins to generate the results of its calculations, and there they are right in the middle of your letter! Between Dear Tom and Sincerely are the gross, net, and percentages of your spreadsheet output. The first time it happens comes as a shock. It seems that we may have lost both letter and spreadsheet data. But not so. Each program is still intact; only that particular screen output got contaminated. To prove this, we save the letter and then reload it. It's still there. Switch back to the spreadsheet in window 1; save and reload the spreadsheet. It's all there with the new calculations in place.

So what looked like a disaster was only a disruption, but who needs these kinds of disruptions? We could use another spreadsheet, one that is well behaved, but we are used to this particular spreadsheet and don't want to give it up. The same is true for your other programs. After all, you bought Concurrent PC DOS to enable you to run your old software and the best of the new.

Well, there is a provision for this situation and it is the SUSPEND command. For programs of the .EXE and .COM type, the SUSPEND command must be entered before the program is loaded and it will then cause that "poorly behaved" program to suspend operation when it is switched out. When you switch it back in again it resumes operation where it left off. SUSPEND works only in the window in which it was entered for .EXE and .COM programs. It stays in effect until you turn it off, or reset or turn off the computer.

To use SUSPEND with programs of the .CMD filetype, you must specify the program name and enter it as a subcommand under the CHSET (set command header) command. This will select that option for that program until it is changed. The syntax is given below.

Program Type	Syntax
.COM,.EXE	A>SUSPEND<ENTER>
(for that session only)	PROGNAME<ENTER>
.CMD	A<CHSET PROGNAME [SUSPEND = ON]<ENTER>
(stays until reset)	

PROGRAM BEHAVIOR CATEGORIES

Now that we have entered the world of the dual operating system environment, we are running programs under one operating system that were designed to run under another. Many times this is not a problem. For example, some programs run just as well under Concurrent as they do under PC DOS. Let's call these type A programs. Then there are those that need only to be suspended when they are switched out. Those are type B.

Then we have a PC DOS program that runs very well but needs just a little tweaking to make it work, perhaps a memory allocation adjustment (using ADDMEM and COMSIZE). Let's call these type C programs. Then there are the programs that break a lot of rules and are very dependent on a certain type of hardware and cannot run in our environment. That's type D. It's too early to tell at this writing what percentage of programs will fall in each category, but Table 8.1 summarizes the overall situation.

TABLE 8.1   **Program Behavior and Adjustments**

Program Behavior Type	Adjustment Needed
A. .COM,.CMD,.EXE	Needs no adjustment
B. .COM,.CMD,.EXE	Needs to be suspended when switched out
C. .COM,.EXE	May need memory adjusted, may need to be suspended, or may have other needs
D. .COM,.EXE	Cannot run because of specific hardware needs

OTHER LIMITATIONS

There are a few other limitations. For instance, you cannot run two programs concurrently that use BASICA.COM, the PC DOS BASIC language interpreter. You also may not be able to run the same program in several windows at the same time. Remember that the amount of memory in your system ultimately dictates how many programs you can run concurrently. Deduct 150K for the operating system from your total RAM and see how many programs you can fit into the rest. Don't forget data.

In order to release the printer from one program to access it from another, you must unload the first program before the second can gain access. Many programs will run on a color monitor but not on a monochrome. Be sure to read the supplement "Running Applications Under Concurrent PC DOS" before you begin.

FILE SYSTEM IMPLICATIONS

Working in a dual-operating-system environment also has implications as to the file systems used in each and for the media formats as well. Table 8.2 summarizes some of the differences between the two file systems. The media differ in that the CP/M file structure allows 320K of storage on an eight-sector double-sided, double-density disk, while PC DOS allows 360K on a nine-sector double-sided, double-density disk. To store programs of both formats on a hard disk, a partition must be created for each. Data files may be moved from one format to the other on either a floppy or hard disk.

Concurrent must be booted from a CP/M-formatted floppy disk or either the DOS or CP/M hard disk partition. PC DOS programs and data may then be used. Since PC DOS floppy disks hold more data, it is efficient to use them as data storage disks. Table 8.2 is a comparison of the features of each type of disk format.

TABLE 8.2   Comparison of File System Attributes

CP/M	PC DOS
User numbers	"Tree" directories
Passwords	"Floating drives"
Time stamping (optional)	Time stamping (automatic)
Archiving	

User numbers are partitions that can be assigned to a floppy disk or a hard disk partition. Unlike "tree" directories, they are linear (i.e., nonbranching). You switch to each user number to see what files are there. Tree directories or hierarchical directories, as they are known, branch from a "root" to successively finer breakdowns of data. You can assign one of the two floating drives (N and O) to a PC DOS root directory or subdirectory.

Time stamping is an automatic feature of the PC DOS format, but it can also be enabled in the CP/M format with the SET command. You can also use the SET command in the CP/M format to establish an archive attribute for files. If the archive attribute is on, it indicates that the file has been backed up. PIP sets the archive bit when you use it to back up only those files that have not been archived (the A option for PIP).

HARDWARE IMPLICATIONS

Using Concurrent PC DOS efficiently will typically require a hard disk machine. However, it can be used on a two-drive system with a bit of careful preparation (see Chapter 3). The minimum RAM requirement listed is 256K. The recommended requirement is 512K. More would certainly not hurt if many large programs are to be run concurrently. A large RAM complement also allows efficient use of an MDisk or memory drive.

CONNECTING OTHER DEVICES TO CONCURRENT

When connecting devices to your computer the most important consideration is the manner in which they receive information. Your computer may communicate with external devices through one of two types of ports, depending on the configuration of the system. The ports are usually optional equipment when you initially purchase your system and you will have to purchase an additional interface card of some sort in order to send information to a printer, plotter, or modem.

The two types of ports are commonly referred to as either a serial port or a parallel port. The single most distinguishing feature between the two is that the parallel port allows eight bytes of data to be transmitted at a single moment, and the serial port allows transfer of a continuous stream of data, byte by byte. There are other differences between the two, including the fact that a serial port allows the computer to receive data as well as to transmit data, but a parallel port only allows the computer to send data to an outside device. The most common type of serial port is the RS-232 port, and the most common type of parallel port is the Centronics port.

Two other important considerations are: the speed of data transmission and the distance over which the data must be transmitted. A parallel port will allow much faster transmission of data because it is sending eight bytes at a time, but the cable through which the data are transmitted should not be any longer than 10 or 12 feet. A serial port, although slower in the transmission of data, can be used with a cable of more than 50 feet and in some cases a cable as long as 150 feet will produce satisfactory data transmission. So the choice is yours, depending on your working environment.

PRINTERS USING CONCURRENT

Concurrent PC DOS will work with either a serial or a parallel printer as long as you have the appropriate interface card installed in your computer. Many printers are available in both versions, although the parallel printer is usually a little less expensive.

One "trick" that you might find useful in getting the most out of your printer is to set your function keys using the FUNCTION command to codes that cause your printer to print in certain styles or "type fonts." Many printers will print in different typefaces or in compressed modes when you precede your printing session with a set of commands called an initialization string. These commands are usually a sequence of characters consisting of an ESCAPE followed by two or more letters. See your printer manual for more information on the specific codes for your machine. In Chapter 10 we discuss the use of the FUNCTION command.

Experiment with the capabilities of your printer to determine its capabilities and then define a batch file that will configure your function keys to the style of printing that you want to use most. Note that many word processors will not allow you to use the function keys to initialize a printer when printing files from them.

Another important thing to remember is that if you are using a serial printer you must set the printer and Concurrent so that they are both receiving data at the same speed, commonly referred to as the "baud rate." You set the baud rate of a port from Concurrent with the SETPORT command (see Chapter 9). The speed of the printer is usually set with switches located on the printer. See your printer manual for additional information.

USING PLOTTERS WITH CONCURRENT

A plotter is a serial device, and the same considerations that we spoke of in hooking up a serial printer hold true for it. That is, you must set the baud rate of the plotter using its switches and set the baud rate of your port using SET-PORT to that same value. Additionally, you may have to set values referred to as parity and stop bits. Again this information is covered in your plotter documentation and in any application software documentation. The most important fact is that they both be set the same.

USING HARD DISKS WITH CONCURRENT

A hard disk requires some special attention when you are using Concurrent. A hard disk usually has an interface card of its own and does not require the use of the ports of the computer. If you have a system with a built-in hard disk, then you will probably not have to do anything to configure your Concurrent for your system. However if you have added a hard disk to your system then you will have to reconfigure with the Field Installable Device Driver (FIDD) provided with the hard disk unit.

Usually, the software provided with the hard disk will consist of the FIDD, which has a filetype of .COM (in this example we call it EXAMPLE.COM), and a file called CONFIG.SYS. You must modify the CONFIG.SYS file with a word processor, such as DR EDIX, in the nontext mode. In that file you will find a statement that resembles

DEVICE = EXAMPLE.COM

You must change this statement to

FIXED-DEVICE = EXAMPLE.COM

where EXAMPLE is the name of the file provided by the hard disk manufacturer. Next, copy both of these files to your boot disk or to the CP/M portion of your hard disk from which you will be booting.

Now replace the CCPM.SYS file on your boot disk with the file provided by Digital Research, named CCPMFIDD.SYS, using this command:

```
PIP D:CCPM.SYS = A:CCPMFIDD.SYS
```

where A: is the source disk and D: is the destination.

USING A MODEM WITH CONCURRENT

A modem is connected to your computer through the serial port. The type of cable that you use with your modem is different from the one that you use with a serial printer. You must be sure to check that you have the correct cable when you buy your modem. The only other consideration in using a modem is that you must set the baud rate of the serial port, using SETPORT, to the proper speed for your modem. After you have done these things, you are ready to start communicating with other computers using DR TALK.

USING A MOUSE POINTING DEVICE WITH CONCURRENT

A mouse is connected to your computer in one of two ways: through your serial port or through a connector on the interface card that is provided with your mouse. See the instructions provided with the mouse that you have. A mouse comes with software to use it with other application programs. Some application programs are written specifically to work with a mouse. Be sure to check the documentation provided with the mouse to see if it will work with the application programs that you have in mind. See discussion of GEM in chapter 9.

9

WHERE DO I GO FROM HERE?

In this chapter we explore some of the more sophisticated additions to Concurrent. We learn how to create a three-user system and some of the ramifications associated with running in a multiuser system.

Probably you first started out interested only in using your computer as a single-user, single-program system. By this I mean that you were the only person using the computer and you were running one program at a time. We've already seen how to do more than one thing at a time using Concurrent's windows. Now let's find out how to generate a system that allows more than one user.

CREATING A THREE-USER SYSTEM

Concurrent directly allows up to three people to use the computer at the same time. However, each user must be able to talk to the computer. In a single-user configuration, you pass commands to the computer through the keyboard and screen, otherwise known as the terminal. Concurrent allows you to connect two more terminals to the computer, much as you would connect a printer to the system. The other two terminals provide the hardware path whereby the other two users can talk to the computer. (Concurrent keeps track of who it is talking to.)

Depending on the hardware configuration of your particular computer system, there will probably be at least one other serial port. (This is similar to the place where you connected your main terminal or console.) So the first step is to connect another terminal to a serial port. We must now make some changes to the characteristics of that port so that we can use the other terminal on it.

You must determine how fast you want your terminal to act. This is known as the baud rate of the terminal. Most terminals allow you to change their baud rates for both input and output. Some have switches, some do it in software. You must look in the instruction manual for the terminal for this information. Also find what the parity and the number of stop bits are. We will need to set these as well. Once you have found this information, run SETPORT to set these values.

SETPORT is menu driven and allows you to modify the serial ports of your computer system. It is intelligent enough to be able to sense how many serial ports you have in the system. If you have none, it will display a message saying so. If you have only one, it will only allow you to change information about one port, and so on. The description in the reference section will fully describe SETPORT. For the time being we will talk about setting baud rates and the like.

If you have not set the port to the proper characteristics for the terminal you intend to hook up to it, strange things will happen. For instance, if the baud rate is wrong, you will not be able to communicate at all. If it is wrong in only one direction (input or output), you will see only one side of a conversation and an incorrect side at that. However, while you must be careful, you will not do any damage. In the case where you don't know some of the information needed, merely change the settings one at a time until the terminal becomes responsive. This is slow and tedious but it works (we have done it several times). (You don't have to reboot the system everytime you change a port value.)

If you are using a modem to communicate, you must set the port baud rate to whatever the baud rate of the modem is. For instance, most modems are 300 or 1200 baud or both. No matter that the terminal can recognize characters at 9600 baud, the modem will not pass them through properly. So you have to set your terminal and the port to the baud rate of the modem.

After you have set the serial port and the terminal so that they can communicate with each other, you need to configure Concurrent so that it uses the serial port as another terminal. Run SETUP to do this.

SETUP will display a main menu to ask you what you want done. Press function key F7 to get us to where we can configure the serial ports. The menu that is displayed at this point tells us how the ports are presently configured (usually they are set up so that the ports are assigned to the printers).

Remember those serial port changes that we made using SETPORT? Well, they are in effect only while power is on to the computer or the system is not rebooted. Once you turn off the power or reboot, those changes disappear and the serial ports will be set back to whatever the old characteristics were. We could reenter the new characteristics every time that we reboot (a smarter way would be to add to the STARTUP1.BAT file the right SETPORT command), or we could save the changes using SETUP.

Return to the main menu of SETUP by using the Esc key. The F3 option asks if you want to save the system parameters. The serial port configuration is included in this. Press key F5 in this submenu to save the serial port configuration and return to the main menu again.

Now that we have finished changing the use of the serial port (from a printer port to a multiuser port), and we have saved the serial port characteristics, you must save the changes in the system image file called CCPM.SYS. SETUP will prompt you for this when you strike function key F10. This submenu asks if you want to save the changes to another disk. Unless the disk in the indicated drive does not have CCPM.SYS on it (or you don't want to change it), just press F5 to change the system image on the default drive. Otherwise, indicate to which drive you want to update the system image. When you change the system image file like this, it is always nice to know that you have a backup of the original disks in case you made an error and can no longer boot the system. Once you save the changes to the system image, you should be out of SETUP and back to where you started.

Now reboot the system with the new terminal added and you should see the Concurrent banner appear on the second terminal. If you don't, we have done something wrong, probably an incorrect terminal setting such as a baud rate. First run SETUP and press the F7 option to find out if Concurrent is using the port as a multiuser terminal. If not, two things may have happened. First check that the CCPM.SYS file that we booted from is actually the file that we thought we changed in SETUP. It is possible that we may have another version of CCPM.SYS on the system. If so, save the old version, copy the new file to the boot disk, and reboot.

The second thing that could have gone wrong is that we did not save the changes properly. (Actually, you may have an older version of Concurrent, where SETUP had a small bug. If the disk that contained the CCPM.SYS that you wanted to change was write protected, SETUP did *NOT* update that disk. Alas it didn't tell you that, leaving you to believe that everything was fine.)

Assuming that the serial port is in fact set to multiuser, verify, using SETPORT, that the port characteristics are what you think your terminal needs. If those are set, we have made a mistake concerning what we think the second terminal needs. Check the manufacturer's manual again and retry.

To recap what you have to do to configure Concurrent as a multiuser system:

1. Read the terminal manual concerning baud rates and such.
2. Run SETPORT to configure the serial port so that it reflects the terminal characteristics.
3. Run SETUP to save the serial port characteristics and to reconfigure the use of the port to a multiuser system.
4. Save the port changes using SETUP to the system image file CCPM.SYS.
5. Test the changes by rebooting.

Another method of making the system multiuser is to use a modem connected to one of the serial ports, so that you can use your computer from some
other place. For instance, you may have a terminal at home with a modem,
and you have a burning need to work after hours at home. By configuring one
of the serial ports as an extra terminal and then connecting a modem to it, you
can dial in to your computer from home and continue to work.

EFFECTS OF A MULTIUSER ENVIRONMENT

Once you have created a multiuser version of the system, you can have other
workers use the main computer. However, there are some trade-offs for the
luxury of having a multiuser system.

Response time will slow down so that there may be noticeable pauses between responses to your work requests. The computer is having to do more work
and can only do so much in any given moment. If the response time becomes
intolerable (a decidedly subjective judgment), perhaps you need a second computer. One of the disadvantages to this alternative is that you might need to
duplicate data files for both machines (and then update both machines so that
the data are timely on both machines). A cheaper solution to poor response
times might be merely to refrain from certain activity during peak periods. Defer
until the evening programs or procedures that consume much of the computer's
resources and make for sluggish response times. Many office activities can be
"saved up" and processed later in one batch or submit file.

Avoid compiling programs when someone else is. Make note of the programs that seem to degrade the system's performance and work out some office rules about when to execute those programs. Sometimes adding memory
or faster peripherals will help. Look closely at what you are doing with your
system and identify the holes.

In Version 3.2 some programs that use the screen in a special manner will
not be able to be run on the second (or third) terminal. The following programs
will run only on the main terminal:

File Manager
DREDIX
EDITMENU
HDMAINT
DRTALK
DSKMAINT
RUNMENU

as well as the menu-driven versions of the following:

FUNCTION
SETPORT
PRINTMGR
SETUP

Any BASICA programs cannot be run when the system is configured for more than one user.

Finally, Concurrent V.3.2 allows you to use only one window on the second or third terminals, while the main terminal still supports four windows.

In version 4.1 however, there are fewer restrictions. Although BASICA programs still cannot be run on a serial terminal, you can run the File Manager, et al., if you have the appropriate TERM.DAT file. These files were introduced in V4.1 to handle different terminal characteristics than the PC keyboard and screen that V3.2 is written for.

MULTIUSER AND FILE UPDATES

Practically all the software that was available commercially in the 16-bit market place at the time when Concurrent was introduced reflects a single-user, single-task operating environment. What this meant was that the writers of the software probably did not design their programs to work when two or more people were using them at one time, particularly when the program updates a file.

Consider the problem of when two people have the same file open and they attempt to write to it at the same time. Who wins? If the software is not designed to be used in a multiuser, multitasking environment, such problems can and will occur.

Starlink

In case a three-user system is still insufficient for your needs, Digital Research also produces another product that is quite closely coupled to Concurrent, called Starlink. With Starlink attached to Concurrent you can expand the maximum number of users to 6.

The Starlink kit is composed of another hardware board, some cables, an instruction manual, and a new set of disks. You must add the new hardware into your system and run some Starlink specific programs to install Starlink on your system. The instructions are quite specific and easy to follow. Be careful that the cables are exactly as described in the Starlink instructions.

Once Starlink is installed, you will have a Concurrent system that is capable of running up to six additional users or talking to four other computers. This is a major step. The ability to network to other Concurrent machines greatly expands the dimensions of your operations without incurring a large learning penalty (the other systems run Concurrent, which you already know).

GEM

If you are in search of a user interface that is even simpler than Concurrent's File Manager menu, then consider Digital Research's Graphic Environment Manager (GEM). GEM allows for the display of computer functions by use of pictures or icons. These icons can be selected and moved between screens using a pointing device, such as a mouse, or the arrow keys found on most IBM PC and compatible keyboards.

GEM requires the use of an IBM or compatible computer with built-in or added graphics capability. There are a number of graphics applications from Digital Research including the following:

GEM Desktop: The main "operating area" screen containing icons representing the programs and files stored on your computer. The Desktop allows you to do most of the operating system functions without the need to type commands. The Desktop includes accessories like a calculator and a clock that are available from pull-down menus like the other operations.

GEM Draw: A drawing package that allows you to create graphics using a variety of line widths and patterns.

GEM Paint: A drawing package similar to GEM Draw, but with greater artistic capabilities.

GEM Write: A graphics-based word processing program based on Volkswriter that allows the merging of text and graphics.

GEM Graph: A program that allows you to create graphics using a pointing device.

GEM WordChart: A program that allows you to create charts using text and graphics.

GEM V1.2 and higher is available for Concurrent PC DOS V4.1.

10

THE CONCURRENT TOOLBOX

Now that we have seen many of the different ways that Concurrent can be utilized to organize your computer work space to conform to your working techniques, let's take a closer look at some of the utilities provided with Concurrent. These utilities allow you to directly control file access, window placement, and disk maintenence. We are not going to attempt to show every possible option of each of these commands, because the purpose of this section is to give you examples of the commands in the form that you will want to use most.

As familiarity with the structure of the operating system grows, you will create files that will set up BATCH files for startup, printer setup, configuring a communication port, function key setup, window management, and file access. This will allow your computer to run the programs that you use on a regular basis in the windows of your choice as soon as you turn on the power to your computer. First let's discuss the concept of the BATCH file.

BATCH FILES

If the last three letters of a file designator are ''.BAT,'' you are working with a BATCH file. A BATCH file is a file that contains a command, or series of commands, that will be executed one after another just as if you had typed them in. You may also pass variables to a BATCH file or include input statements, but for our purposes we will concern ourselves with the creation of files that will set up the computer to our usual working situation with no additional input.

To create a BATCH file, you must use a text editor such as DR EDIX. You may also use the word processor that you are most familiar with in the

nondocument mode or use the COPY command. To create a file called SAM-
PLE.BAT with COPY, enter the command

COPY CON: SAMPLE.BAT

Each line that you enter at the console after this command will be added
to the file SAMPLE.BAT until you press a Ctrl-Z followed by <ENTER>. You
may not edit any text that you are entering when using this technique except
to back up and delete within a line. One important thing to keep in mind when
creating a BATCH file is that each statement will be executed in the order in
which you place it in the file. It is also important to remember that each line
must be followed by pressing the <ENTER> key to create a file that will function correctly.

THE STARTUP PROCEDURE

When you start your computer, Concurrent searches for several different
BATCH files. It doesn't matter whether you are booting from a floppy or
a hard disk; the same procedure is followed. First, the operating system executes a command in each of a series of files. The first is STARTUP1.BAT (for
window 1) followed by STARTUP2.BAT, STARTUP3.BAT, and
STARTUP4.BAT until it has checked for a file for each of the four windows.
It is recommended that you use STARTUP1.BAT for all your windowing commands (more on those soon) and that you use the other files to change the
DIRECTORY level and to execute the programs that you want to run in each
window. As you feel more and more comfortable with Concurrent, you will
see the logic in this technique.

THE WINDOW MANAGER (WMENU)

Use of the WMENU command will provide you with an interactive method of
creating and saving the size of windows. Among the attributes that you will
be able to set are size, placement, and colors. You may then save these attributes
to a file so that they are sized correctly when you start your computer.

When you choose one of the WMENU options a description of the commands available to you appears on the screen. With the exception of a few items,
the commands are self-explanatory. Let's discuss some of the ways that you
can use these commands in your work.

To set up the BATCH files that will create your windows when you start
your computer, install the Window Manager by typing WMENU. Next press
Ctrl + and select the SIZE command. Use the arrow keys to size each window
(when you have sized one window, switch to another and size it). Return to the
main menu and position each window on the screen (the PLACE option).

TABLE 10.1 WMENU Commands

Command	Description
PLACE	Moves the window on the screen
SIZE	Reduces the size of the window by raising the bottom or moving the right border to the left
SCROLL	Enables you to move the window on the screen, showing different areas of the text below it
TRACKING	Determines whether the window is locked over the position of the cursor
DISPLAY	Lets you choose between a black-and-white monitor, color monitor, or both
WRITE	Lets you create files of the WINDOW configuration or a text file of the window contents
ABORT	To leave WMENU

When you finally have your screen configured to your liking, save the configuration to a BATCH file with the WRITE command. To do this, execute the WRITE command and use the arrow keys to create a file called WSETUP.BAT. You may rename this file to STARTUP1.BAT if you want your computer to be configured in this manner when you start your computer. In a short while we will reexamine this file.

Note that you may also save the contents of any window to a text file with the WRITE command. If the window is a partial one, if you select the WINDOWn.TXT (n stands for the window number) option of WRITE, then WMENU will only save in that file an image of the text that you can see in that window. Thus, if the text in the window is truncated or cut off, that is what is written to WINDOWn.TXT. If you were in a full-screen window, this option would show the entire screen. You can, however, still get a picture of what the entire screen would show when your window is smaller than the entire screen. Use the CONSOLEn.TXT file option of WRITE and WMENU will copy the window to the file as if it were a full-screen window.

You may bring this text into any text file that you are creating with your word processor. This is a particularly valuable feature for moving information that you have generated from your spreadsheet or information that you have received through your modem to your word processor.

WMENU works in an interactive mode; that is, you load it and then you can control it during normal keyboard execution. What if you wanted to control the windows but were running a BATCH-type program? Concurrent has supplied a program called WINDOW that provides the same services as WMENU except that you invoke it through a command line interface. Unlike WMENU, which is installed until you ABORT it, WINDOW must be installed every time you use it. Therefore, you cannot talk to it at will through a special key sequence (Ctrl +); it does not filter the keyboard input.

THE WINDOW CHANGE COMMAND

One of the subcommands of the WINDOW command is WINDOW CHANGE. It is this command that you use to set up your windows in STARTUP1.BAT. Let's use one of the case studies from Chapter 7, that of the microcomputer programmer. This particular example had the screen split into two large windows and one smaller window, with another process running in the background. Refer to Figure 7.2 to see what the screen in this example actually looks like. Now let's see what the BATCH file that created this window looks like:

```
WINDOW CHG N = 3 PR = 1,PC = 1,NR = 24,NC = 80,VR = 1,VC = 1,TR = ROW,FG = WH,BG = R
WINDOW CHG N = 1 PR = 1,PC = 1,NR = 10,NC = 80,VR = 1,VC = 1,TR = ROW,FG = WH,BG = R
WINDOW CHG N = 2 PR = 12,PC = 1,NR = 10,NC = 80,VR = 1,VC = 1,TR = ROW,FG = WH,BG = R
WINDOW CHG N = 4 PR = 23,PC = 1,NR = 2,NC = 80,VR = 1,VC = 1,TR = ROW,FG = WH,BG = R
```

To understand what is going on in this file, examine the first line of the BATCH file. The first two character strings, WINDOW CHG, invoke the WINDOW CHANGE command, and the characters following are the parameter list. The first parameter is the window number, N = 3. In this particular example we have started by defining window 3 because it is a background process, and when we define the remaining windows they will overlap window 3.

Following that is the row and column at which the window will begin, PR and PC. In this example the window for this console is a full screen, so we start at row 1, column 1. This is the upper left corner of the screen. Following those values are the number of rows and columns that are part of the window, NR and NC. For these values we use the numbers that represent a full screen: number of rows = 24, number of columns = 80.

The last two parameters, FG and BG, are for the foreground and background colors. The foreground color is set to white and the background color is red. It is not necessary to include these parameters in a startup file unless you want something other than white foreground and black background. See Chapter 11 for a complete list of the color choices. The next three lines of the batch file follow the same format as the one we just discussed.

Remember the file we created through WMENU, called WSETUP.BAT? Well, WSETUP.BAT looks exactly like the last example, the only changes being the actual values (depends on how you sized your windows). You can rename WSETUP.BAT to STARTUP1.BAT and add any additional commands to get your windows configured automatically every time you boot Concurrent.

DIRECTORIES

Once you have set your windows, the next step is to set each window to the level of DIRECTORY where the program you wish to run is located. Let's talk about directory structures at this point.

The names of the files on a disk are located in an area of the disk called the directory. Also in this area are indicators as to some of the attributes of those files, including file size, and the location of the data. If you execute a program, the first thing that occurs is that the operating system checks the directory of the currently logged-in disk to see if a command file of that name exists. If it does exist in that directory, it will load and run the program.

So far we are speaking of file directories on a one-dimensional level, but there may be multiple levels in any directory. Different operating systems have their directories organized in different manners. CP/M and DOS both have ways to access different levels of directories, but they are very different from each other.

Concurrent has the ability to work within the framework of the directory structures built into both CP/M and PC DOS. Before we discuss the utilities we must examine how the directories are actually organized. The concept of directories as supported by CP/M is best illustrated as shown in Figure 10.1. In this particular representation the directory called "user 0" is shown as being directly available to any of the other directories or "user areas." Actually, for a program or data file that exists in user 0 to be accessible to another user area, the file attribute "SYSTEM" must be set. This means that in any CP/M media any file that exists in user 0 and is set to SYSTEM may be accessed from any other user area. To set the system attributes, the Concurrent command SET is used. To SET all the files in user 0 to SYSTEM, enabling them to be accessed from all other user areas, you would use the following command:

SET *.*[SYS]

Now let's discuss the structure of the DOS directories. DOS directories are organized into an "inverted tree" structure in which you may add as many subdirectories to the root as disk space will allow. Let's start again with an illustration of a possible DOS directory. Figure 10.2 shows three levels of directories; actually, you could continue the progression of creating lower levels of directories as far as you like until you run out of directory space.

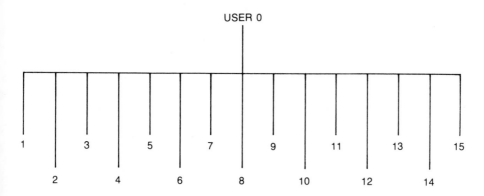

Figure 10.1 CP/M User Area Structure

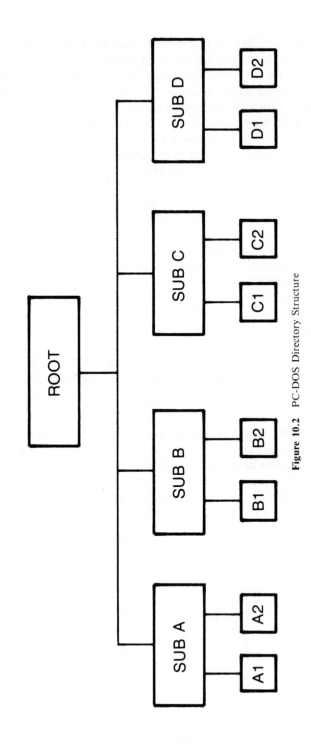

Figure 10.2 PC-DOS Directory Structure

You may only access the files that are in the level of directory that you are logged into unless you have used SYSDISK to set another directory as the system disk. The system disk is that directory where Concurrent searches for the command file if it doesn't find it in the current directory. As we mentioned before, on CP/M media all files that you want to be available from other user areas must be marked SYSTEM and be in user 0. For PC DOS media, the file must be marked SYSTEM.

SYSDISK is a utility that lets you change or interrogate the currently assigned system disk. If you type in SYSDISK without any command tail, Concurrent will display the path name of the current system disk. A path name describes each node in the directory hierarchy in complete detail. For instance, using the directory structure above, a valid path name would be

root\suba

The "\" separates each directory node. As we read the path name from left to right, we can see that it describes the route or path we used to get to the files (or directories) under the directory "sub a." If we had further levels to descend, we would append the names of each directory until we got the directory we wanted. A path is much like a road map that gives us directions to a particular node in the directory structure. Notice that we can have directories with the same name in our structure as long as the path name is unique! For instance, we could have a directory called TEST under both SUBA and SUBB because the path names would be different: ROOT\SUBA\TEST versus ROOT\SUBB\TEST. The same thing applies to filenames (TEST could also be a filename).

Now the node or directory that we wish to designate as the system disk must be specified using SYSDISK in the following manner:

A>SYSDISK C:\SUBA

We do not need to specify the root directory because the first backslash "\" right after a drive name means the root directory on the drive. Thus "C:\" means "C:\ROOT." In this case we have told Concurrent that if it cannot find the program in the current directory, go look in the SUBA directory on drive C. What about specifying a system disk for CP/M? Essentially the same method is pertinent. For instance, if we want drive D, user 0 to be the system drive, we use the command

A>SYSDISK D:\

Because CP/M does not support hierarchical directories, Concurrent interprets this command to mean drive D, user 0. You cannot specify a user area other than 0 as a system drive.

DIRECTORY-RELATED UTILITIES

DIR

One of the most useful utilities when dealing with directories is DIR. DIR lists the files and subdirectories, if they exist, that are currently accessible to the end user from the console at which he or she executes the command. You may use a drive specifier with the DIR command if you want the directory of a drive other than the current drive. In addition, you may search for a specific file by including it in the command.

Here is an example of the command line required to search for a file called PHONELST.DAT on the default drive:

DIR PHONELST.DAT

If you prefer, you can search for all files with a filetype of DAT by using the wildcard "*":

DIR *.DAT

SDIR

This is another command used to generate a list of the files that are accessible to you. SDIR allows you to do more things than DIR. The most visible difference between SDIR and DIR is that SDIR lists the files in alphabetical order, and lists additional attributes, including:

The size of the files
The number of records in each file
Whether you can write to that file
The date of creation
The date of most recent update

You may still use the same wildcard in your selective search. Consult Chapter 11 for more information on the SDIR options.

USER

With the USER command you can determine which user area you are in when on a CP/M disk. You can move from one user area to another with the USER command by passing a parameter such as

USER 12

With this particular command you would change the directory level to user 12.

Remember that if you are on a CP/M disk and you are in a user area other than 0, the prompt will tell which user area you are in: that is,

3B>

for user 3, drive B.

There are several other commands that are used with tree-structured directories. The following utilities are used for creating, deleting, or changing directories when using DOS media.

MKDIR

MaKe DIRectory is the utility used to create a subdirectory. The easiest way to use it is to create a directory in the current directory. If you were in the LAW directory and wished to create a subdirectory called MARITAL, use the command

MKDIR MARITAL

You may realize by now that you could create a subdirectory called SMITH in the MARITAL directory by moving to the MARITAL directory and creating it. You can also create it while still in the LAW directory by specifying the subdirectories that you must move through (the path) as in this command:

MKDIR MARITAL\SMITH

RMDIR

If you are finished with a directory and want to get rid of it, you cannot delete it with the ERA or ERASE command, but you can delete it with the ReMove DIRectory command. Before you can delete a directory you must erase all the files in that directory. Other than that, the same rules follow as when creating a directory. You must specify the subdirectories if you wish to delete a directory that is not in the current directory. If you were still in the LAW directory and wished to delete the SMITH subdirectory that was created above, you would use the following command:

RMDIR MARITAL\SMITH

Keep in mind that you will receive an error message if you have not erased all the files in SMITH or if you give an incorrect path through the subdirectories. Also, you cannot delete the directory you are in, nor a directory above you in the path name.

CHDIR

We have created directories with MKDIR, removed them with RMDIR, and now we will move from one directory to another using CHDIR. If you are in the LAW directory and want to change to the MARITAL directory, you could use the command CHDIR as in this example:

```
CHDIR MARITAL
```

Again, the same rules apply in changing directories that applied in creating them. You may specify a path to a specific directory if you choose to, as in this example:

```
CHDIR MARITAL\SMITH
```

CD is another way of running CHDIR. Thus

```
CD MARITAL\SMITH
```

is another valid way of changing directories.

Concurrent has several assignable directories that are called "floating directories." By assigning one of your PC DOS media subdirectories to one of your floating drives, you may access it at any time. See the discussion of moving files under the COPY command in this section.

SYSDISK

SYSDISK was explained above during our discussion of directory structures. However, there is something about using SYSDISK that should be made clear. If you change the system disk to something else, in order to execute a special set of programs, trying to run your normal set of programs (those files that you have on your normal system disk) will not work unless you fully specify the path name when you try to run the program.

For instance, assume that your normal system disk is drive D, user 0, and you have loaded all of Concurrent's utilities in this user area (set to SYSTEM). Notice that this is a CP/M disk. Suppose that you want to run a compiler that runs under PC DOS and that it resides in a subdirectory on drive C. So you create a BATCH file in drive D to use when you want to use that compiler, for example,

```
SYSDISK C:\COMPILER
ERASE $1.OBJ
COMP $1
```

Notice that the first command in the BATCH file changes the system disk to a subdirectory on drive C. What do you suppose happens when the second instruction is executed? Right. Unless there is a program called ERASE on drive C, subdirectory COMPILER, Concurrent will fail to erase the specified object file. And if you do not restore the system disk to what it was when you began the BATCH job, you might find yourself lost in the directory structures. So let's change our BATCH file to

```
SYSDISK C:\COMPILER
D:ERASE $1.OBJ
COMP $1
D:SYSDISK D:\
```

Notice that we had to fully specify the path where Concurrent could find both ERASE and SYSDISK (because we changed the path).

OTHER FREQUENTLY USED COMMANDS

The last group of commands that we will examine in this section are those that pertain to general file and disk maintenance functions. This includes the copying or examination of files and the formatting of disks:

SHOW

This command returns information on the status and characteristics of your disk drives. The most common use of SHOW is to determine the amount of space available on your disk drives. You may also use SHOW to determine the user areas that have files in them on CP/M media, the disk label, and information on the format of information on your drives. To display the amount of available space on all your logged-in drives, use the command

```
SHOW SPACE
```

You may also use a drive specifier to determine the amount of available space on a specific drive, as in this example:

```
SHOW D:SPACE
```

This example would show the available space on drive D.

COPY

This command is used to copy files from one disk to another or from one user area to another. To copy the file SAMPLE.TXT from drive A to drive D, use the command

```
COPY A:SAMPLE.TXT D:
```

Notice that the source file is always specified first, and then the destination. You may also copy it to a file of another name, as in this example, which produces a copy of SAMPLE.TXT named SAMPLE.SAV on the same drive:

COPY SAMPLE.TXT SAMPLE.SAV

While Concurrent supports the directory structure of PC DOS, it is still an inherently CP/M system and has a flat directory structure to work with. This means that in order for it to simulate the working environment of a hierarchical directory structure, it must use some tricks, like floating drives.

A floating drive is a device that Concurrent uses solely to handle movement of files from one subdirectory to another. Concurrent uses drives N and O as floating drives, which means that you can assign these drives to some path name so that you can move files out of one subdirectory to another. Upon system startup, drives N and O are assigned to the system drive, but you can change them to fit your needs by using the CHDIR command:

CHDIR N: = C:\LAW\MARITAL

If you listed the files on drive N after executing the command above, you will see the files in the LAW subdirectory. Now what if I wanted to move a file from the root directory to C:\MARITAL\LAW (and the current directory is the root directory on drive C)? Use drive N as if it were a real drive and type the command

C>COPY SAMPLE.TXT N:

We could also have copied files from N to C by

N>COPY TORT.TXT C:

Each window maintains its own floating drive assignments, so you can have drive N assigned to something entirely different in window 2 as in window 1. You can also copy files to the default printer (LST:) and the console (CON:).

PIP

This is another file copying utility with a number of differences. One of those differences is that you may use PIP to copy from one user area to another. Notice that with PIP the destination precedes the source. To copy a file from drive D, user area 12 to drive D, user area 1, use the command

PIP d:[g1] = d:SAMPLE.TXT[g12]

Remember that USER has no meaning on DOS media, so you are generally better off using COPY if you are working on DOS media. Floating drives work in the same fashion as described above.

Finally, before we leave this section we need to discuss the utilities that are used to format your disks.

DSKMAINT

This is the utility used to format floppy disks. It may also be used to copy from one floppy disk to another. It is entirely menu driven and is self-explanatory. Type the command DSKMAINT to examine this utility.

HDMAINT

This is the utility used to format your hard disk. It can also change how your hard disk is partitioned. Like DSKMAINT it is entirely menu driven and merely typing the command HDMAINT will lead you through a series of commands that will tell you how to format your hard disk. You usually format your hard disk only once, as formatting it will erase all data stored on it.

Warning: Reformatting or changing the partition of your hard disk will cause the loss of data and files, so be sure to back up all files before using HDMAINT.

This concludes our discussion of some of the major utilities that go to make up your Concurrent toolbox. The best way to become familiar with these utilities and the others not covered in this chapter is to experiment on your own.

11

READY REFERENCE:

CONCURRENT PC DOS COMMANDS

The following are brief descriptions of the Concurrent PC DOS utility programs that are included with the system. For a fuller treatment of the major commands and how they are used together, see Chapter 10. For the fullest description of options and parameters, see the "Concurrent PC DOS User's Guide" that accompanies the product. Several commands are resident in the operating system. This means that they are available as long as the operating system is loaded. Also, they take up no RAM when they run. The resident commands are

ADDMEN	ORDER	STOP	8087
COMSIZE	PRINTER	SUSPEND	
DIR	RUNMENU	USER	

8087

Used to tell Concurrent that the next program to be run will require the 8087 coprocessor. Also used to disable the 8087 coprocessor when not needed. If an 8087 coprocessor is not installed, a message will be reported to that effect and the program will not run. The syntax is

$$8087 = ON$$
$$8087 = OFF$$

ADDMEM

Used to allocate additional memory to programs that require it. To see how much memory is allocated, enter the command alone. To add additional memory, type in the amount (0–999) after the command and an equal sign. The syntax is

ADDMEM

ADDMEM = n

BACK

Used to make floppy disk backup copies of files from your hard disk. You can back up an entire partition or selected files by specifying a control parameter such as a filetype. Using the CONTROL parameter makes BACK take its directions from a CONTROLx.BR file. The letter x stands for the last character in the filename—the way a specific CONTROL file is identified. You may want to have several different ones. You can get a report sent to the printer by using the REPORT subcommand after the BACK command. The syntax is

BACK

BACK FULL

BACK CONTROL = x

BACK REPORT

BATCH

Used to submit a chain of commands as a single command. You create a batch file with a word processor or text editor and give it a filetype of .BAT. You can enter up to 10 options (0–9) with a BATCH command. You can also use the subcommands PAUSE and REM to embed remarks of up to 121 characters. These can be displayed as messages or prompts during a pause or continuously as the BATCH command is processing. You can also nest BATCH files if you use the second syntax line. The syntax is

filename.BAT {option 1. . . .option 9}

BATCH d:filename {option 1. . . .option 9}

CARDFILE

An application program that creates a small data base of your name and address file that can be accessed under Concurrent either through the command line or through the File Manager. If you have a color monitor, you must specify the color option. The syntax is

CARDFILE

CARDFILE COLOR

CHDIR

Used to assign names and floating drives (fd:) to subdirectories as well as, when used alone, to display the current subdirectory path on a given drive. The command may also be abbreviated to CD. The syntax is

```
CD
CHDIR
CHDIR {fd:} {d:} { \ }
CHDIR {fd:} {d:} = directory pathname
```

CHSET

Used to display or modify the command header of any .CMD-type program. Entered alone, it brings up helpful information about the command. Entered with a filename, it displays that file's current command header settings. Also used to supend operation of CMD programs in "switched-out" windows. The syntax is

```
CHSET
CHSET {:d} filename
CHSET {d:} filename [option = setting, option = setting . . . }
```

Option	Settings
8087	ON, OFF, OPTional
SHARED	ON, OFF
SUSPEND	ON, OFF

COMSIZE

Used to increase or decrease the memory allocation in your current window for .COM-type programs. Entered alone, it displays the current allocation. Entered with a value (0–999), it sets the allocation to that value in kilobytes. The syntax is

```
COMSIZE
COMSIZE = n
```

COPY

Used to copy files between disk drives, devices, and directories. COPY is of DOS origin as opposed to PIP, which is similar but of CP/M origin. In COPY, the source information is given first followed by a space and then the destination information. The basic syntax is

```
COPY source destination
COPY source/option destination/option
```

Options are:

Option	Function
/A	Treats as ASCII file
/B	Copies whole file
/V	Verifies the copy
/n	Denotes user number (CP/M media only)
+	Indicates source files are to be concatenated

Device	Descriptions
CON:	Console, (i.e., keyboard and screen); when used as input device, it refers to the keyboard; when output, it refers to the screen
LPT1:	Currently assigned printer
NUL:	Nonexistent dummy device assignment used for testing
PRN:	Same as LPT1:

COPYMENU

Used to copy menus between menu files. Used with the other menu commands (EDITMENU, RUNMENU) to allow the user to create, modify, and manipulate custom-made menus. When used with the -M option, copies all existing menus. To specify a subset, provide a list of menus to be copied. Sample syntax is

```
COPYMENU
COPYMENU source destination -M
COPYMENU source destination menulist
```

DATE

Used to set the month, day, and year for the internal clock. Usually used with the TIME command to provide time and date stamping whenever a file is created, accessed, or updated. (CP/M media require that the INITDIR and SET commands be run first.) If used alone, the command shows the current date setting and prompts for a new one. The basic syntax is

```
DATE
DATE mm/dd/yy or mm-dd-yy
```

DEL

This command is an abbreviation for DELETE, another name for the ERASE command (*which see*).

DEL   file   specification

DELQ

This stands for "delete with query." Another version of the ERASE command that asks the operator for confirmation before deleting a file. Useful when deleting a number of files. *See also* ERAQ.

DELQ   file   specification

DIR

Used with or without options to list the contents of a directory. When followed by a filename, it confirms or denies the presence of that file in the directory. Options are: /S, to show files with the system attribute; /L, to show the length of the file and (if enabled) the time and date the file was last accessed; and /P, to show only one page (screenful) at a time. The basic syntax is

DIR
DIR d:
DIR filename
DIR d:filename
DIR d:filename/options

DREDIX

This command is used to run the Concurrent text editor.

DREDIX

DRTALK

This command is used to run the Concurrent communications utility.

DRTALK

DSKMAINT

Used to format new or reusable disks to accept data, copy entire disks, or verify the readability of data on a disk. Care must be taken to use the same kind of disks (single- or double-sided, eight- or nine-sector) when copying. Otherwise, the destination disk will have to be reformatted to the same format as the source disk, thus erasing all files, if any, on the destination disk. DSKMAINT will not operate if there are files open in windows other than the current one. After entering the command a menu shows the function keys that will run the options as well as one that provides HELP.

DSKMAINT

ERAQ

Used to erase files. Similar to ERASE but queries the operator for confirmation before erasing. Especially convenient when erasing a large number of files. You can enter ERAQ *.* and selectively erase from the resulting list rather than have to enter each filename. Also used (with the XFCB option) to erase previously set passwords. The syntax is

ERAQ filename
ERAQ filename [XFCB]

ERASE

Used to erase files from a disk directory. It will accept wildcard characters and will prompt the operator for confirmation when * is used. The command can be abbreviated to ERA.

ERASE filename

FM

This command runs the File Manager program, which allows you to perform many operations (copy, type, print, etc.) with your files by means of a menu-driven screen display rather than having to use the command line.

FM

FUNCTION

Used to assign specific commands to the function keys and the numeric keypad keys. You can also use it to change the window-switching keys if they interfere with the running of a program. Function keys must be defined for each window. They can also be defined in batch files that load a given program and relate specifically to that program. When the command is entered alone, a menu of options is presented. The syntax is

FUNCTION
FUNCTION {d:}filename.PFK

HDMAINT

Used to format a hard disk or to create, modify, or delete a partition. Also used to determine which partition is bootable, verify data, and display or change directory information. Documentation of this utility is found on disk in the file HDMAINT.DOC.

HDMAINT

HELP

Displays information about Concurrent system commands on line. When the command alone is entered, a menu of command names is displayed. When the command is entered with a topic, information on that topic is presented. Subtopics and examples are also available. Customized HELP files can be created by means of several options supplied. The syntax is

HELP
HELP topic {subtopic . . . }
HELP [option]

INITDIR

Used to prepare CP/M media for time and date stamps. (On DOS media, this happens automatically.) Enter the command followed by the letter of the drive containing the disk to be formatted and the password, if any. You must then use the SET command to turn on time and date stamping. The syntax is

INITDIR d:

LOADCCPM

Used to load Concurrent from a DOS partition on a hard disk. By using the "ask" option, the system will prompt you whether you want to load Concurrent or PC DOS. The syntax is

LOADCCPM
LOADCCPM ASK

MKDIR

Used to create subdirectories on PC DOS media. If you insert a backslash before the first subdirectory entry, the subdirectory will begin at the root directory of the specified (or default) drive. If no backslash is used, the current directory is used. The command can also be abbreviated to MD.

MKDIR {d:}{\} directory path

ORDER

Used to display or change the filetype search order. Concurrent searches for files in the following order: CMD, COM, EXE, BAT. To change this, list the filetypes in the order you would like them to be searched after the command. Using the command alone will display the current search order. The syntax is

                         ORDER
                         ORDER type1, type2,..4

PIP

Used to copy files between disk drives, directories, and certain devices. Multiple operations may be entered if the command is typed in without parameters. PIP is of CP/M origin and is somewhat more powerful than COPY, which does the same thing but is of DOS origin. PIP must be used to move files between user numbers on CP/M media. PIP requires that the destination information be entered first followed by an equal sign and then the source information. Sample syntax is

                    PIP
                    PIP destination {[Gn]} = source[options]

Option	Function	Option	Function
A	Archives	O	Combines object code
C	Confirms	Pn	Page length n lines
Dn	Deletes past column n	Qs	Quits copy after string s
E	Echos to screen	R	Reads system files
F	Filters form feed characters	Ss	Starts copy from string s
Gn	User number n	Tn	Spaces tabs by n
H	Transfers hex data	U	Makes copy all uppercase
I	Ignores :00 records	V	Verifies copy
L	Makes copy all lowercase	W	Writes over read only
N	Adds line numbers	Z	Zero parity bit

PRINTER

Used to display or set the printer assignment for a given window. When the command is entered alone, the system responds with the current printer assignment. To change an assignment, enter the printer number with the command. The syntax is

                         PRINTER
                         PRINTER n

PRINTMGR

Used to print multiple copies of a file, print simultaneous files from different windows, or to print a file while running another program in the same window. PRINTMGR has seven subcommands and nine options available. Once the process has been started and printers designated, you can specify margins, page length, tabs, and so on, for the files to be printed. The syntax is

PRINTMGR subcommand
PRINTMGR filename filename. . .[option,option. . .]

Subcommand	Function
DEL n	Deletes entry n from print queue
H	Displays HELP summary of options
PRINT	Prints the files specified
RES	Resets the Printmanager
STAR n	Starts the system for printer n
STAT	Displays system status
TER	Terminates the system

Option	Function
COP = n	Prints n copies
FOR	Formats to 55 lines/page
FORM = n	Sets document length to n lines
MAR = n	Sets left margin to n spaces
NOF	No form feed between files
NUM	Numbers each page after 55 lines
PAGE = n	Prints n lines per page
PRI = n	Sends file to printer n
TAB = n	Makes every nth column a tab

REN

Used to rename files. A drive must be specified if the file is not on the current drive. Wildcard (?,*) characters can be used in filenames. If the file to be renamed has a password, you must specify it to be able to rename the file. If you specify a new name that is already in use, the file is not renamed and a message to that effect is sent to the screen. The command can be abbreviated to REN. The syntax is

RENAME (d:)oldfilename newfilename

REST

Used to restore files to a hard disk that were backed up with the BACK command. CONTROLn.BR files specify the information used to regulate the restoration process. A printed report is generated at the end of the process. By using the REPORT subcommand, you can request a printed report of previous restore operations. The syntax is

```
REST
REST CONTROL = n
REST REPORT
```

RMDIR

Used to remove a specified subdirectory in other than the current or a floating drive. The directory may not contain any files or other subdirectories (except for . and ..). The command can be abbreviated to RD.

```
RMDIR {d:}directory path
```

RUNMENU

Used to bring up a menu from a menu file. Menufiles have names and the menus within them also have names. If you do not specify a menufile name, MENU.DAT is assumed. If you do not specify a menu by name, MAIN is assumed. The menufile must be in the current directory. The syntax is

```
RUNMENU
RUNMENU menufile
RUNMENU menufile menuname
```

SDIR

When entered alone, SDIR displays all files by name and file type, their size in bytes and records, their attribute assignments, whether or not they are password protected, and the date and time that each file was created (optional with CP/M media). Files are listed alphabetically and totals are given for bytes, blocks, records, and files. The number of directory entries used (out of total available) is also shown. You can specify a subset of files with or without wild-card characters (?,*) or by filetype, attribute, password, or user number. Other options are possible. The syntax is

```
SDIR
SDIR filename, filename,.,,
SDIR option, option...
SDIR filename,option...
SDIR option, filename, filename,...
SDIR filename,filename,...,option
```

Option	Function
DIR	Directory attribute
SYS	System attribute
RO	Read-only attribute
RW	Read/write attribute
DR = a	Shows all drives
DR = d	Shows drive d
U = a	Shows all user numbers
U = n	Shows user number n
L = n	Shows n lines of display between headings
SI	Shows size of each file in k
FF	Sends a form feed and, if L is set, after every n lines
M	Sets error message for empty directories
XFCB	Shows only password-protected directories
NONX	Shows only those files not password protected
NOS	Shows files not sorted
E	Shows files excluded by specifications entered

SET

Used to set attributes for file or disk read/write access, archival file backup, directory/system access, passwords for files and disks, and labels for disks. Also used to initialize password protection and time and date stamping on CP/M media after initializing with INITDIR. The syntax is

SET [options]
SET d:[option = setting]
SET d:filename [option = setting]

Option	Settings	Function
ACCESS	ON, OFF[a]	Records file access dates
CREATE	ON, OFF[a]	Records file creation date
DEFAULT	password	Set default password
NAME	diskname	Puts name on disk
PROTECT	ON,OFF	Enables protection
PROTECT filename	READ, WRITE, DELETE, NONE	Sets protect mode
PASSWORD	password	Sets password
PASSWORD	<ENTER>	Deletes password
UPDATE	ON, OFF	Records date of last file change

[a]ACCESS and CREATE cannot both be enabled at the same time.

File or Drive Attribute	Function
RO	Read only
RW	Read/write
SYS	System attribute
DIR	Directory attribute
ARCHIVE	Archive attribute

SETPORT

Used to display and change the characteristics of the serial ports. These ports are used to communicate with printers, plotters, modems, and separate terminals. Up to two terminals can be connected to the computer under Concurrent PC DOS to permit multiuser capability. You must know the requirements of the devices that you want to install before using SETPORT. If the command is entered alone, a menu displays the current values and tells the user how to change those values. If the command is entered with values specified, they are entered directly bypassing the menu. These settings are in effect only until the computer is reset. To make them permanent, the SETUP command must be run. The syntax is

SETPORT
SETPORT values

Parameter	Values
Baud rate	110, 150, 300, 600, 1200, 2400, 4800, 9600
Word length	5, 6, 7, 8
Parity	ODD, EVEN, NONE
Stop bits	1, 2
Protocol	
I	Input side of port
O	Output side of port
D	DSR/DTR on
R	RTS/CTS on
X	XON/XOFF on
N	Turns option off

SETUP

Used to display and change certain system parameters. Entered alone, the command brings up a series of menus from which you change these parameters. You can bypass the main menu by entering an option preceded by a slash mark.

This takes you directly to the option menu specified. SETUP values are recorded in CCPM.SYS and are read every time the system is started.

SETUP
SETUP /option

Option	Function
HEAD	Diskette head step time
MEMORY	Maximum memory for a process
MDISK	Specifies size of RAM disk
PARAM	Saves system parameters
PFKSAVE	Saves programmable function keys
PORTSAV	Saves serial port values
SERIAL	Selects serial console
VERIFY	Verifies after diskette write

SHOW

Used to display file and drive information for a specified drive or, when the command is entered alone, the current drive. Options are available that can also show user numbers in use and what files are in them, drive labels, password status, and other characteristics. The HELP option provides a summary of command syntax.

SHOW
SHOW d:
SHOW d: option, option...

Option	Function
DRIVE	Disk drive recording values
HELP	Displays command syntax
LABEL	Shows drive label, protection status, time and date label created
SPACE	Shows space remaining on drive
USERS	Shows all user numbers with files

STOP

Used to display the name of programs running in all windows, their size in kilobytes, as well as which window they are in. The user is prompted to enter an entry number after a prompt to stop a given program. When the command is entered with a program name and window number, the program is stopped immediately, bypassing the display and prompt.

```
STOP
STOP program n
```

SUSPEND

Used to suspend temporarily operation of a COM or EXE program (use CHSET for CMD programs) while in a switched-out window. A suspended program resumes operation when its window becomes switched-in. This command must be entered in the appropriate window before the program it is to control is run. It remains in effect until it is turned off or the computer is reset. This process is required because certain programs go around the operating system and send output directly to the screen. Under Concurrent, these programs must be suspended so that they do not interfere with those running in other windows. The syntax is

```
SUSPEND = ON
SUSPEND = OFF
```

SYSDISK

Used to display or define the system disk drive and to enable or disable the filetype search sequence (see the ORDER command). If the search sequence is turned off (SYSDISK OFF), Concurrent searches only the current drive or directory of the one you specified. If you turn it back on (SYSDISK ON), this feature resumes searching the current drive/directory and the system drive/directory for CMD, COM, EXE, and BAT files. When Concurrent is started it has a default system disk and filetype search order shown above. You can change the system disk to any disk drive, even a RAM disk, drive M: (see the SETUP command), or PC DOS root directory or subdirectory. The syntax is

```
SYSDISK
SYSDISK d:
SYSDISK d:\directory path
SYSDISK ON
SYSDISK OFF
```

TIME

Used to display or set the internal clock of the computer. Concurrent displays the time at the far right-hand side of the status line. It also uses the internal clock to time stamp files if you have enabled this function. When the computer is started, the clock is at midnight (00:00:00) and begins counting on a 24-hour cycle (i.e., 5 P.M. is 17:00). Therefore, the clock will show the time elapsed since last reset only if you do not set it when you begin a session. You enter the command alone to display the time and to be prompted for a change, or the command and your new value to change it directly. The syntax is

```
TIME
TIME hh:mm:ss.00
```

TYPE

Used to display a text file on the screen and also have it printed. You must use the filename, filetype, and password (if any) in the specification. No wild-card characters (?,*) are accepted. If you enter a Control-P before TYPE, the file will be sent to the printer as it scrolls on the screen. Another Control-P will stop the printer. To stop the scroll, enter a Control-S. Control-Q will let it resume. The syntax is

```
TYPE d:filename.type;password
```

USER

Used to display the current user number or log into a different user number. User numbers apply to CP/M media only. PC-DOS media uses sub-directories to organize files. When you start Concurrent, it comes up in user 0. Zero is not displayed in the system prompt, but all the other 15 possible user numbers appear before the system prompt when you are logged into them (e.g., 3B, 12A). To find out which user numbers are in use, use the SHOW command (SHOW USER) and it will show you how many files are in which user numbers. The syntax is

```
USER
USER n
```

WINDOW

Used as a command line mode to display and modify window parameters. WMENU is the menu-driven interface to the window management system. The following subcommands are available under WINDOW: View, Top, Full, WRite, CHange. They can be abbreviated to the uppercase letters shown. After the subcommands are entered, the parameters are to be changed. Besides viewing, manipulating, and changing any of the four windows, you can write the contents of a window to a file. Sample syntax for the command is

```
WINDOW View
WINDOW Top N = n
WINDOW Full N = n
WINDOW WRite N = n TYPE = C,FILE = d:filename.type
WINDOW CHange N = n FGColor = BLUe BGColor = BLAck
```

Subcommand	Function
CHANGE	Alters a window's parameters
FULL	Shows entire window
TOP	Brings specified window to full screen
VIEW	Shows each window's current values
WRITE	Copies contents of a window to a file

Window Change Parameter[a]	Values
PRow	1–24
PCol	1–80
NRows	1–24
NCols	1–80
VRow	1–24
VCol	1–24
TRacking	ROW, NO
Display	COLOR, B&W
FGColor and BGColor	BLAck, BLUe, CYan, Green, Magenta, Red, White

Window View Parameter[a]	Values
Number	Window number
PRow	Number of physical row of top border of window
PCol	Number of physical column of left window border
NRows	Number of rows in that window
NCols	Number of columns in that window
VRow	Number of virtual scroll point row
VCol	Number of virtual scroll point column
TRacking	Window contains the ROW of the cursor or NO
Display	Indicates that output is going to a color or black-and-white monitor
FBColor	Foreground color of screen
BGColor	Background color of screen

Window Write Parameter[a]	Values
Number	Window number
TYPE	Window, Console, or Setup
FILE	File name

[a]May be abbreviated to capitals.

WMENU

Used to interactively change window parameters. Entering the command installs the window manager. Pressing Ctrl + (the plus key on the numeric keypad) brings up the command menu on the bottom of your screen, replacing the status line. This also dedicates the numeric keypad for WMENU commands. (It is best to do this before running programs in other windows.) By using the arrow keys on the keypad and the RETURN key, you can now select and change parameters. WMENU will also create files that record the current parameters of all windows (type S), record the contents of a given window (type W), and record the full program display (type C). The files are written to user 0 on CP/M media or to the current PC DOS directory on the current drive. The window configuration saved as a type S file can be restored by entering the file WSETUP.

WMENU

Subcommand	Function
ABORT	Stops WMENU
COLOR	Sets background and foreground colors
DISPLAY	Selects for a color of monochrome monitor
PLACE	Moves a window's left and top borders
SCROLL	Allows positioning of a window
SIZE	Moves a window's right and bottom borders
TRACKING	Permits cursor tracking or not
WRITE	Creates a file of commands, displays, or contents of a window

Write Option	Function
S	Records current parameter values of all windows in a WSETUP.BAT file
W	Copies the contents of window n in a WINDOWn.TXT file
C	Copies entire screen contents into a Consolen.TXT file

APPENDIX A

Common Abbreviations

ADDMEM   Command used to ADD MEMory to an EXE file
Alt   ALTernate shift key
ANSI   American National Standards Institute
ASCII   American Standard Code for Information Interchange, a standard character set
AXI   AuXiliary port 1 (one)
AXO   AuXiliary port 0 (zero)
BACK   Command used to BACKup hard disk files
.BAT   BATch file filetype
BATCH file   An executable file that contains commands batched for sequential execution
BDOS   Basic Disk Operating System
BG   BackGround color
BIOS   Basic Input/Output System
Bit   BInary digiT
.BR   Back/Rest control file filetype; file contains backup parameters
CD   Further command abbreviation of CHDIR
.CFG   ConFiGuration file filetype; file contains configuration settings
CHDIR   Command used to CHange DIRectories
CHSET   Command used to CHange SETings in the command header of .CMD files
.CMD   CoManDfile filetype; file contains an executable program
.COM   COMmand file filetype; represents an executable program file
COMSIZE   COMmand that adjusts the SIZE of .COM files
CON: CONsole designation
COPY/UPDT   COPY UPDaTe command in Cardfile program
CP/M   Control Program for Microprocessors
CRT   Cathode Ray Tube (terminal)
Ctrl   ConTRoL key

.DAT DATa file filetype; file contains data only

Del DELete key

DEL Command used to DELete files

DELQ Command used to DELete files and Queries for confirmation for each entry

DEV DEVice

DIR Command that displays DIRectories

Dirname DIRectory NAME

Dirpath DIRectory PATH; path of subdirectories

DOS Disk Operating System

DR EDIX Digital Research EDIX, Concurrent's text editing program

DR TALK Digital Research TALK, Concurrent's communication program

DSKMAINT Command that facilitates DiSK MAINTenance

DSP DeSPooler program; command that stops the print SPooLer

.EDX EDiX file filetype; used with DR EDIX

EOF: End Of File mark (Ctrl-Z)

ERA Command that ERAses files

ERAQ Command that ERAses files and Queries for confirmation for each entry

Esc ESCape key

.EXE EXEcutable program filetype; represents an executable program file

FCB File Control Block

FD Floating Drive

FG ForeGround color

Filespec FILE SPECification

FM The File Manager program included with Concurrent

HDMAINT Command that facilitates Hard Disk MAINtenance

.IDX InDeX file filetype; used with Cardfile

INITDIR Command to INITialize DIRectories to accept time/date stamps (CP/M media)

Ins INSert key

I/O Input and Output functions referred to collectively

K Kilobyte, 1024 bytes

.KEY Function KEY filetype; file contains function key assignments

LPT: Listing PrinTer currently assigned

LST: LiST device

MD Further command abbreviation of MKDIR

MDisk Memory DISK, a virtual disk drive created in RAM to speed processing for certain purposes

MKDIR Command to MaKe subDIRectories on DOS media

.MNU MeNU file filetype; file contains menus that can be executed

NUL: NULL designation, dummy device assignment

Numlock Key that locks the numeric keypad into numeric mode and disables cursor control; when turned off, cursor control returns

.PCT Filetype of the SCReeNDUMP file; contains a PiCTure of screen contents

.PFK Programmable Function Key file filetype; file contains function key assignments

PgDn Key to move one PaGe DowN in sequence

PgUp Key to move one PaGe UP in sequence

PIP Command for the Peripheral Interchange Program, the CP/M copy utility

PRINTMGR Command for the PRINT ManaGeR utility program

PRN: Current PRiNter assigned
PrtSc PRinT SCreen key
RAM Random Access Memory, the computer's active work area
RAMDISK Random Access Memory DISK; *see* MDisk
RD Further command abbreviation of RMDIR
REM REMark; an explanation embedded in a program or command; *see also* BATCH
file
REN Command for the file REName utility
REST Command for the hard disk file RESToration program; used after BACKing
up files
RMDIR Command to ReMove subDIRectories on DOS media
RO, R/O Read Only; file cannot be written to
RW, R/W Read/Write; file can be read and written to
SDIR Command to display the Status DIRectory
SPL SPooLer program; holds files for sequential printing
.SYS SYStem file filetype
SYSDISK Command to display or assign the SYStem DISK and the filetype search
sequence
TMP Terminal Message Processor
.TRM TeRMinal setting filetype; file contains the default settings of the terminal
.TXT TeXT file filetype; file contains ASCII text characters
WMENU Command to invoke the Window MENU for setting window parameters
XFCB Option that allows SDIR to display only files that are password protected
XIOS The eXtended Input/Output System
XMODEM Communications error-checking protocol
XOFF Communications signal indicating buffer full, not accepting data
XON Communications signal indicating "ready to receive"

APPENDIX B

GLOSSARY

ADDMEM   Command used to allocate additional memory to .EXE programs. See Chapter 11.

Append   To add something to the end of another thing.

Arrow Keys   Keys that display arrows on them and are used to position the cursor on the screen.

ASCII Collating Sequence   A standard sorting sequence that contains not only the alphabet but other symbols and characters in an established order.

BACK   Command used to back up hard disk files on floppy disks. See Chapter 11.

Background   As opposed to foreground. The surrounding field of something that stands out from that field.

BATCH   Command used to group a chain of commands and submit them once for sequential processing. See Chapter 11.

Baud Rate   Used to indicate the speed of transmission of characters. Typically refers to bits per second (bps).

Buffer   Anything that stores information temporarily while waiting for some action to be performed on it.

CARDFILE   A small data base program included with the Concurrent PC DOS operating system that allows the filing of names, addresses, and telephone numbers.

CHDIR   The command used to display or assign names to subdirectories or "floating drives" on PC DOS media only.

CHSET   Command used to display or change the command header of a .CMD program. See Chapter 11.

Command   The name of a program (usually abbreviated) that the computer recognizes as its signal to make it run that program.

Command Line   The sequence of characters in precise syntax that tells the computer exactly what to do. *See also* User Interface.

Command Tail   The set of options entered after a command to specify precisely how it will be executed.

COMSIZE   Command used to display or change the memory allocation in the current window of a .COM program. See Chapter 11.

Concatenate   To attach one thing to the end of another.

Concurrency   The ability of a computer to process several jobs at the same time. *See also* Multitasking.

Console   Collective term for a device that has a keyboard and a video screen. One of four operational subsections of the Concurrent PC DOS operating system. *See also* Terminal.

Contiguous   Making contact at a point or along a boundary.

Control Keys   A key that is used in connection with another key to create a new "key." Much like the shift key on a typewriter that allows you to create uppercase letters when held down.

COPY   Command used to reproduce files or even create files. See Chapter 11.

COPYMENU   Command used to copy menus between menu files. See Chapter 11.

Cursor   Character that appears on the screen to indicate where the input you type in will appear.

Cursor Movement Keys   Those keys on the numeric keypad that can also be used to position the cursor when the Numlock function is not active. *See also* Arrow Keys.

Cylinder   Used to define a storage area on a hard disk. Refers to the area described by tracks that are used for a common purpose and that are stacked on disk platters in the same position on each track. Created as the multiple read/write heads access data at the same time on the multiple surfaces of several platters of the overall disk.

DATE   Command used to display or set the date the system uses to date stamp files. See Chapter 11.

DEL   Command used to delete files. See Chapter 11.

DELQ   Command used to delete files that queries (asks) you to confirm your intentions before it executes. See Chapter 11.

Device   A computer component such as the keyboard, screen, disk drive, printer, and so on. Usually categorized as either input or output.

DIR   Command used to display the names of file(s) contained in a directory. See Chapter 11.

Directory   A list of filenames that may also contain other information about the files.

DR EDIX   A text editing program included with Concurrent PC DOS that is used for file creation and editing as well as word processing.

DR TALK   A communications program included with Concurrent PC DOS that allows one computer to talk to another. Derived from the popular PC TALK.

DSKMAINT   Command used to format disks to receive data as well as to copy and verify data between disks. See Chapter 11.

Enable   To ready something for work.

ERAQ   Command used to erase files that queries (asks) you to confirm your intentions before it executes.

ERASE   Command used to erase files from a disk directory. See Chapter 11.

Execute   To cause a program to run.

Filename   The eight-character name of a file, usually followed by a three-character extension.

Filespec   The filename plus drive designator, filetype, password: the entire specification of the file.

Foreground   Those features of a field that stand out as opposed to being in the background.

FM   Command abbreviation for the File Manager, a directory management program included with Concurrent PC DOS.

FUNCTION   Command used to assign or change the function and "window-switching" keys. Entered alone, it brings up a menu. You can also enter assignments with the command. See Chapter 11.

Function Keys   Keys that can be defined to execute different functions in different programs or environments.

Global   Relating to the entire file or programming environment.

HDMAINT   Command used to create or modify hard disk partitions. Documentation of this utility program is found in a text file on disk 5 of the Concurrent PC DOS disk set.

HELP   When loaded, this reference utility displays information about system commands. You can also add information of your own to the file.

Hierarchical   Relating to a hierarchy, having a structure of elements subordinated under other elements, usually referring to the DOS operating system file structure.

INITDIR   Command used with CP/M media to prepare it for time and date stamps. See Chapter 11.

LOADCCPM   Command used to load the operating system from a DOS partition on a hard disk. See Chapter 11.

Logical   Formally accepted as true. Dealing with the principles and interrelations of internal computer functioning. An MDisk is a "logical" disk drive.

Menu   A list of options presented to a user on the screen making possible the execution of a function without typing in a command.

Menu Driven   A user interface that consists of a series of menus.

MKDIR   Command used to create subdirectories on PC DOS media. See Chapter 11.

Multitasking   Capable of handling several processes simultaneously in one computer processor. *See also* Concurrency.

Null   A zero setting or dummy operation in which there is no effect. Used to test software routines.

ORDER   Command used to display or alter the system filetype search order. See Chapter 11.

PIP   Command used to copy files between directories and devices. See Chapter 11.

PRINTER   Command used to display or make a printer assignment to a given window. See Chapter 11.

PRINTMGR   A program that manages all printer output from Concurrent PC DOS. It allows simultaneous printing from different windows; it allows multiple copy printing; it also allows sequential printing by means of a print queue.

Redirection   Taking input or output from its usual course and routing it to another destination.

REN   Command used to rename files. See Chapter 11.

REST Command used to restore backed-up files to a hard disk. Used in conjunction with the BACK command. See Chapter 11.

RMDIR Command used to remove a subdirectory. See Chapter 11.

RUNMENU Command used to bring up a menu from a menu file and execute it. See Chapter 11.

Screen The physical video display to be distinguished from windows.

SDIR Command used to display filenames, sizes, and attributes. More comprehensive than DIR. See Chapter 11.

SET Command used to assign read/write access privilege to files and disks. See Chapter 11.

SETPORT Command used to display and change the configuration of a serial port. You must know the requirements of the device you wish to attach to a serial port before you can configure the port successfully. See Chapter 11.

SETUP Command used to display and change certain system settings. See Chapter 11.

SHOW Command used to display drive and file information. See Chapter 11.

STOP Command used to display and/or stop programs running in windows other than the one this command is running in. See Chapter 11.

Submit File A file of commands grouped so that they can be executed at once in a certain order.

SUSPEND Command used to suspend operation of .COM or .EXE programs so that they do not send output to another window while they are switched out. See Chapter 11.

SYSDISK Command used to display or assign the system drive and enable the ORDER command; *see* ORDER. See also Chapter 11.

Terminal Originally consisting of a printer and a keyboard and used primarily for teletype transmission. The term now refers to consoles as well.

TIME Command used to display or set the internal clock of the computer. Used with the DATE command; *see* DATE. See also Chapter 11.

Tree Directory A directory structure that looks like an inverted tree (or root structure) in which subordinated elements "branch" from major ones.

TYPE Command used to display (on screen) or print (on a printer) a text file. A Ctrl-P must precede the command to enable the printer. See Chapter 11.

USER Command used to display or change the current user number on CP/M media. See Chapter 11.

User Interface That part of the operating system that interprets what the user does into what the machine can understand. This means interpreting what you enter with a keyboard, mouse, light pen, etc.

User Numbers In CP/M media, a method of grouping files together in numbered (0–15) "areas" for convenience of access.

Virtual Acting as if . . . . Used to define something that is treated as if it were potentially something else.

Wildcards Characters that can stand for many other characters in designating files. The most popular are "?", which stands for any character in a given place, and "*", which can stand for many characters in a field.

Window Used to define the area in which a task is being executed in. Also called a virtual console. Similar to a channel on a TV set, in which a "program" runs autonomously in an area separate from other channels.

WINDOW   Command used to display or change window settings with command line entries. WMENU allows menu-driven changes; *see* WMENU. See also Chapter 11.

WMENU   Command that, in turn, invokes a subcommand menu replacing the status line. Changes in window settings are made interactively by means of this menu. See Chapter 11.

APPENDIX C

CONCURRENT SYSTEM MESSAGES

When you do something wrong or something goes wrong with the hardware, the operating system gives you a message to that effect. These messages are generated from several sources: an operating system command that you are using, the Basic Disk Operating System (BDOS) itself, the eXtended Input/Output System (XIOS), and so on. These messages are listed here with brief explanations of the probable cause and/or suggestions for remedy. Sometimes the message will "quote" the file or process name or other data you specified or that it needs in the message itself. We have included these "quotations" in square brackets. Parentheses indicate alternative versions of identifying terms. Messages are also grouped by common explanation when possible.

The form of these messages has been edited for consistency, so they may vary slightly from what appears on the screen. The source of the message is also included so that you can look in Section 8 of the operating system user's guide documentation for further clues to the problem.

8087 not installed
> You tried to turn on the 8087 coprocessor but it is not properly installed or is missing. (8087)

A file system error was encountered while reading the file.
> The disk is probably bad. Try using another copy of the file. (PRINTMGR)

A Print Manager is already set up on this system.
> You tried to load the Print Manager twice. (PRINTMGR)

Backup and hard disk media types differ, can't restore.

> You reformatted your hard disk since the last backup. (back/REST)

Bad disk

> The disk you are attempting to write to has its protection notch covered or is defective. (DSKMAINT)

Bad pattern

> The pattern you specified to search contains an illegal character. (DR EDIX)

Bad sector on disk

> This indicates that the disk you are using is probably defective. (FUNCTION)

Bad target

> You selected an illegal destination for moving copy. (DR EDIX)

Cannot execute under this operating system version.

> You tried to run this utility under a different version of the operating system other than the one with which it was intended to run. (HDMAINT)

Cannot execute while any files are open.

> No other programs can be running when this program does. (HDMAINT)

Cannot execute without a hard disk.

> Either there is no hard disk in your system or it is defective. (HDMAINT)

Cannot find CPM.SYS or CCPM.SYS.
Try another diskette.

> Either Concurrent is not on the disk that you loaded or the disk is defective.

Cannot properly initialize the disk you inserted,
Please remove it and insert a new CP/M (DOS) media disk.
Touch RETURN key when ready = = =>

> You tried to use a disk that was write-protected, defective, or unformatted. (BACK/rest)

Cannot write to reserved system area
Cannot read the reserved system area

> Probably indicates a defective area on the hard disk. Try to move partition boundaries. (HDMAINT)

Cannot write to partition table
Cannot read the partition table

Probably indicates a defective hard disk. Check power and connections or have unit serviced. (HDMAINT)

Can't allocate memory
You don't have enough memory to run this program. You will have to stop another program to make room for this one. (RUNMENU)

Can't create [filespec]
There's not enough disk space left to create this file. (DR EDIX)

Can't create new file
There's not enough disk space left to create a new file. (RUNMENU)

Can't find CCPM.SYS
This program is not on the drive you are searching. (SETUP)

Can't find DOS partition
You have not yet established a DOS partition on the hard disk. Restart Concurrent and use HDMAINT to do so. (LOADCCPM)

Can't find file: CPM.SYS/CCPM.SYS
The hard disk loader cannot find the Concurrent operating system file (or the CPM system file) in the CPM partition on the hard disk. Boot Concurrent from the floppy disk and carefully install it again on the hard disk.

Can't find DOS file: CCPM.SYS
The hard disk loader cannot find the Concurrent operating system file in the DOS partition on the hard disk. Boot Concurrent from the floppy disk and carefully install it again on the hard disk.

Can't find specified menu
The menu program cannot find the main menu or the one you specified. Enter the command again carefully. (RUNMENU)

Can't load CCPM.SYS—Input/output devices are now in use by a MODE, ramdisk, or spooler command.
You have executed an I/O redirection command and then tried to load Concurrent. This is not possible. Load Concurrent first before you enter any such commands. (LOADCCPM)

Can't open [filespec]
Can't open [filespec]; new file assumed
The file you are attempting to access cannot be opened.
Check spelling or drive location. (DR EDIX)

Can't open menu file
A menu file cannot be found where you have specified. Check spelling or drive location. (RUNMENU)

Can't read CCPM.SYS
> The disk or disk drive is probably defective. Read Appendix D.
> (SETUP)

Can't read from boot disk
> The hard disk loader cannot read the operating system file in the DOS
> partition. Try loading Concurrent again from floppy disk. If that
> fails, try to recreate your DOS partition. Otherwise, you probably
> have a hardware problem.

Can't read menu
Can't read source menu
> The system cannot read the menu file specified or the default file
> MENU.DAT. Check spelling or disk. Try another copy of the menu
> file. (COPYMENU, RUNMENU)

Can't remove subdirectory
> The subdirectory you are trying to remove still contains files. Remove
> them before trying to erase the subdirectory. (RMDIR)

Can't write destination menu
> The disk is probably defective or full. Try another disk.
> (COPYMENU)

Can't write to CCPM.SYS
> This message probably indicates a defective disk, disk drive, or other
> hardware problem. See Appendix D. (SETUP)

Concurrent error: Bad sector
> This indicates a probable disk, disk drive, or other hardware prob-
> lem. Refer to Appendix D. (REName,SET)

Concurrent error: Bad file spec
Concurrent error: Bad disk drive | filename | file ext. | password
> The file specification you entered contains one or more errors. Reenter
> the file specification. (TMP)

Concurrent error: Can't find BATCH.CMD
> The batch command has to be accessible before you can run a batch
> file. Copy it to your current drive. (TMP)

Concurrent error: Can't find command
> Check spelling or disk to see if command is there. If not, copy it to
> your current drive. (TMP)

Concurrent error: CLI abort
> You stopped the command line interpreter with a Ctrl-C. Reenter
> your command. (TMP)

Concurrent error: File not found
>Check spelling or disk to see if file is there. (TMP)

Concurrent error: Invalid drive specification
>Check your drive designation. You have specified a disk drive letter that is not one of those recognized (i.e., A–H, M, N, O, and P).

Concurrent error: Load error
>The program or command you are trying to run is probably defective. Try a backup copy. If that fails, you may need service on your hardware. (TMP)

Concurrent error: Not enough memory
>If you receive this message and your system still has unallocated RAM, you can allocate it to the process you are trying to run. If not, you will have to stop some other process to load a new one. *See also* ADDMEM, COMSIZE, and SETUP. (TMP)

Concurrent error: PD table full
>This indicates that you are trying to load more programs or commands than your computer can handle. You will have to stop something in order to load anything new. (TMP)

Concurrent error: Read error
>This indicates a probable disk, disk drive, or other hardware problem. Refer to Appendix D. (TMP)

Concurrent error: RSP command queue full
>The command you entered is executing in another window. You will have to wait or stop it before trying to use it somewhere else. (TMP)

Concurrent error on [d]: Close checksum error
>The file you are trying to close does not exist on the disk, the disk has not been reset, or the program running is not certified for use with Concurrent. Reboot Concurrent and try the same thing again with no other programs running. (BDOS)

Concurrent error on [d]: Disk I/O
>This indicates a probable disk, disk drive, or other hardware problem. Refer to Appendix D. (BDOS)

Concurrent error on [d]: Disk reset denied
>This indicates that a file is open in some process and your current process is trying to reset the drive. Wait for the file to be closed or stop it in order to do the disk reset. (BDOS)

Concurrent error on [d]: File already exists
>There is already a file with that name in the current directory. Use a new name. (BDOS)

Concurrent error on [d]: File currently open
> This indicates that a program tried to modify a file that has been opened by another program. Wait until the file is closed or stop that program. (BDOS)

Concurrent error on [d]: File opened in Read-Only mode
> This indicates that a program has tried to write to a file that is write protected. That file must be closed and reset to read/write mode. (BDOS)

Concurrent error on [d]: Illegal ? in FCB
> You have attempted to use a wildcard character in a file control block where it is not permitted. Rename the file. (BDOS)

Concurrent error on [d]: Invalid drive
> You specified a drive that is not one of those that Concurrent recognizes (i.e., A–H, M, N, O, and P). (BDOS)

Concurrent error on [d]: No room in system lock list
> The system lock list cannot accommodate any further entries. (BDOS)

Concurrent error on [d]: Open file limit exceeded
> This indicates that a program has attempted to exceed the maximum number of files per process that can be opened. (BDOS)

Concurrent error on [d]: Password error
> You specified a password that is incorrect or you failed to present a password. Check spelling or acquire correct password. (BDOS)

Concurrent error on [d]: Read-Only file
> This indicates that a program has tried to write to a file that is write protected. That file must be closed and reset to read/write mode. (BDOS)

Concurrent error on [d]:
> This indicates that a program has tried to write to a file on a drive that is write protected. That drive must be reset to read/write mode. (BDOS)

Could not interpret parameters in WINDOW CHANGE command
> Check syntax or spelling in your WINDOW command line. (WINDOW)

Could not obtain access to a Print Manager in the system
> Check to see that the Print Manager is loaded and that at least one printer is specified. (PRINTMGR)

Could not open file [filespec]
> Check spelling or whether another process is using that file or whether that file is in the directory you are logged into. (PRINTMGR)

Could not protect or reset drive
>That disk drive is probably defective. See Appendix D. (SET)

CP/M system area is defective
>This message flashes when Concurrent cannot gain access to the CP/M partition on your hard disk. It indicates a serious hardware failure. If you already have files in the partition and cannot gain access by repeated tries, you will have to create a new CP/M partition, thus erasing all files in the current one. (HDMAINT)

Concurrent is already loaded
>You attempted to load Concurrent on top of itself. This cannot be done. You can proceed. (LOADCCPM)

Defective DOS file: CCPM.SYS
>The operating system file in the DOS partition of your hard disk is defective. Reload Concurrent from the floppy disk and copy it anew to the DOS partition. (Hard Disk Loader)

Defective hard disk CP/M partition
>The hard disk system loader can no longer detect a CP/M partition. Load Concurrent from floppy disk and recreate the CP/M partition. All files on the previous partition will be erased. (Hard Disk Loader)

Destination backup drive [d]: has a Read-Only file,
Please remove it and insert a new [CP/M or DOS] media disk.
Touch RETURN key when ready = = =>
>Check the destination drive disk for read-only files. Use SET to make them read/write. Make sure that the disk's write protect notch is uncovered. (BACK/rest)

Destination backup drive [d]: has a sector error,
Please remove it and insert a new [CP/M or DOS] media disk.
Touch RETURN key when ready = = =>
>The destination disk is defective. Replace it. (BACK/rest)

Destination is not a hard disk
>You did not specify the PC DOS hard disk partition. Reenter your command. (REDOS)

Destination is R/O, Delete (Y/N)?
>The destination file specified is read-only and cannot be updated or overwritten. You can save it and thus have two versions or delete it and retain only the new version. (PIP)

Destination Menu Directory Full.
Press F10 to continue with the copy function or press Esc to abort.
>You must delete a menu from the specified menu file to make room for any new ones or create a new menu file. (COPYMENU)

Device full
> The destination disk is full. Erase files to make room for more or use another disk. (DR EDIX)

Directory already exists
> You have tried to create a subdirectory with a name that is already in use on that drive. (MKDIR)

Directory full
> The destination disk is full. Erase files to make room for more or use another disk. (FUNCTION)

Directory needs to be reformatted for time/date stamps
> You must use INITDIR to initialize a CP/M directory before you can set time/date stamps on it. (SET)

Disk error Drive [d]: Track 00 [variation] Retry, Ignore, Accept?
> This message has a great number of variations. They are listed below and are inserted appropriately after the track information. In general, this message means that Concurrent has encountered difficulty reading from or writing to a disk. (XIOS)

Disk Error Message Variations

Address mark missing	Illegal command
Bad address mark	No address mark
Bad disk controller	No response
Bad track flag set	Operation timeout
Can't reset disk	Read CRC
Can't sense status	Read doesn't match
Controller failed	Record not found
Data corrected	Reset failed
Data error	ROS command error
DMA address error	Sector not found
DMA chip failure	Seek failed
Drive setup error	Sense op failed
Drive parameters	Track flag error
Error not defined	Uncorrectable data
Failed to respond	Undefined error
Head position error	Write-protected

Use the "Retry" option if you can find the problem and correct it. You can then resume your work. Using "Ignore" returns you to the operating system at the point you were before you entered the error condition. If the error condition is not corrected, you can get the message again when you duplicate those conditions. "Accept" also returns you to the operating system and presents you with a "Concurrent error" message.

Disk I/O error
> This indicates a problem somewhere in the hardware itself. See Appendix D for a list of possible problems and suggested remedies.

Disk error in reading CCPM.SYS (CPM.SYS)
Disk error reading DOS file: CCPM.SYS
Disk error reading system loader
> Your CP/M or DOS hard disk partition is defective. Restart Concurrent from diskette and recreate that partition with HDMAINT after deleting all files. If the problem persists, your hard disk may need repair.

Disk full
> Use a new disk or erase unnecessary files to make room for the file you are trying to create. (FUNCTION)

Disk not ready
> This disk cannot be read. Check the drive to see if it is open or if the disk has been put in correctly.

Divide interrupt from [process] at [memory address]
Press any key to stop process
> A program has performed an illegal operation. Concurrent must be restarted. (XIOS)

Drive read only
> You must reset this disk drive to read/write in order to rename your file. (REName)

DSKMAINT cannot run in the background
> You cannot switch windows while running this utility. (DSKMAINT)

DSKMAINT cannot run while there are open files on any of the drives
> You must close all files on all drivers in order to run this utility. (DSKMAINT)

Empty buffer
> You attempted to delete the last line in the buffer. That is not allowed. (DR EDIX)

Empty delete stack
> You tried to undo something you didn't do. There is nothing in the delete stack to undelete. (DR EDIX)

Enable password protection first: SET [d]:[protect = on]
> You tried to set a password on a file without enabling password protection. (SET)

Entry number too large
> You tried to stop a process but used the wrong number. Use only the numbers displayed in the STOP menu. (STOP)

Error found on disk.
Please remove it and insert a new CP/M (DOS) media disk.
Touch return key when ready = = = >
> The disk is defective. Replace it. (BACK/rest)

Error loading operating system
> Your hard disk partition is defective. Restart Concurrent from diskette and recreate that partition with HDMAINT after deleting all files. If the problem persists, your hard disk may need repair.

Error reading control file.
> The CONTROL.BR file is defective. You must replace it or recreate it. (BACK/REST)

Error while closing file [d]:[filespec]
> The utility was unable to close the file or was interrupted in the process. (CHSET)

Error while reading system file
Try another diskette
> Use a backup copy to load the operating system file CCPM.SYS. The current file cannot be read.

Error while writing file, check disk. (Press any key to continue.)
> The disk may be write protected (notch covered) or full. (WMENU)

Error writing menu, COPYMENU Abort
Error writing menu, EDITMENU Abort
> The disk is either full or defective. (COPYMENU, EDITMENU)

ERROR: BAD PARAMETER
> You have specified an illegal option. (PIP)

ERROR: CAN'T DELETE TEMP FILE [d]:[filespec]
> This indicates a probable disk or other hardware problem. Refer to Appendix D. (PIP)

ERROR: CAN'T DELETE TEMP FILE INCOMPATIBLE MODE—
[d]:[filespec]
> You are trying to delete a temporary file (.$$$ type) that is in use by another process. It must be closed before it can be deleted. (PIP)

ERROR: CAN'T DELETE TEMP FILE INVALID PASSWORD—
[d]:[filespec]
> You used the wrong password in an attempt to delete this file. (PIP)

ERROR: CAN'T DELETE TEMP FILE NONRECOVERABLE—
[d]:[filespec]
> This indicates a probable disk drive or other hardware problem. Refer
> to Appendix D. (PIP)

ERROR: CAN'T DELETE TEMP FILE R/O DISK—[d]:[filespec]
> The disk drive must be SET to read/write before this file can be
> deleted. (PIP)

ERROR: CAN'T DELETE TEMP FILE R/O FILE—[d]:[filespec]
> The file you are attempting to delete is set to read only and must
> be SET to read/write before it can be deleted. (PIP)

ERROR: CLOSE FILE—[d]:[filespec]
> This indicates a probable disk or other hardware problem. Refer to
> Appendix D. (PIP)

ERROR: CLOSE FILE FOR CHECKSUM—[d]:[filespec]
> This indicates a probable disk, disk drive, or other hardware prob-
> lem. Refer to Appendix D. (PIP)

ERROR: CLOSE FILE INVALID DISK SELECT—[d]:[filespec]
> You specified an unacceptable drive designation. Those accepted are
> A-H, M, N, O, and P. (PIP)

ERROR: CLOSE FILE NONRECOVERABLE—[d]:[filespec]
> This indicates a probable disk, disk drive, or other hardware prob-
> lem. Refer to Appendix D. (PIP)

ERROR: CLOSE FILE R/O DISK—[d]:[filespec]
> You must SET the disk drive to read/write before you can write to
> it. (PIP)

ERROR: CURRENTLY OPENED
> You have attempted to reSET a file that is open. You must close the
> file before using SET with it. (SET)

ERROR: DISK READ—[d]:[filespec]
> This indicates a probable disk or other hardware problem. Refer to
> Appendix D. (PIP)

ERROR: DISK READ CAN'T CLOSE CURRENT EXTENT—
[d]:[filespec]
> This indicates a probable disk, disk drive, or other hardware prob-
> lem. Refer to Appendix D. (PIP)

ERROR: DISK READ FCB CHECKSUM—[d]:[filespec]
> This indicates a probable disk, disk drive, or other hardware prob-
> lem. Refer to Appendix D. (PIP)

ERROR: DISK READ INVALID DISK SELECT—[d]:[filespec]
You specified an unacceptable drive designation. Those accepted are
A-H, M, N, O, and P. (PIP)

ERROR: DISK READ INVALID FILENAME—[d]:[filespec]
Check the file name you have entered. It must be only eight characters
long and use only acceptable characters. (PIP)

ERROR: DISK READ NONRECOVERABLE—[d]:[filespec]
This indicates a probable disk, disk drive, or other hardware problem. Refer to Appendix D. (PIP)

ERROR: DISK READ RANDOM RECORD OUT OF RANGE—
[d]:[filespec]
This indicates a probable disk, disk drive, or other hardware problem. Refer to Appendix D. (PIP)

ERROR: DISK READ SEEK TO UNWRITTEN EXTENT—[d]:[filespec]
This indicates a probable disk, disk drive, or other hardware problem. Refer to Appendix D. (PIP)

ERROR: DISK WRITE—[d]:[filespec]
This indicates a probable disk, disk drive, or other hardware problem. Refer to Appendix D. (PIP)

ERROR: DISK WRITE CAN'T CLOSE CURRENT EXTENT—
[d]:[filespec]
This indicates a probable disk, disk drive, or other hardware problem. Refer to Appendix D. (PIP)

ERROR: DISK WRITE FCB CHECKSUM—[d]:[filespec]
This indicates a probable disk, disk drive, or other hardware problem. Refer to Appendix D. (PIP)

ERROR: DISK WRITE INVALID DISK SELECT—[d]:[filespec]
You specified an unacceptable drive designation. Those accepted are
A-H, M, N, O, and P. (PIP)

ERROR: DISK WRITE NO DATA BLOCK—[d]:[filespec]
The destination disk is full. Erase files to make room for more or
use another disk. (PIP)

ERROR: DISK WRITE NO DIRECTORY SPACE—[d]:[filespec]
The destination disk directory is full. Erase files to make room for
more or use another disk. (PIP)

ERROR: DISK WRITE NONRECOVERABLE—[d]:[filespec]
This indicates a probable disk, disk drive, or other hardware problem. Refer to Appendix D. (PIP)

ERROR: DISK WRITE R/O DISK—[d]:[filespec]
> You are trying to write to a read-only disk drive. Use SET to make the drive read/write. (PIP)

ERROR: DISK WRITE R/O FILE—[d]:[filespec]
> You are trying to write to a read-only disk file. Use SET to make the file read/write. (PIP)

ERROR: DISK WRITE RANDOM RECORD OUT OF RANGE—
[d]:[filespec]
> This indicates a probable disk, disk drive, or other hardware problem. Refer to Appendix D. (PIP)

ERROR: DISK WRITE RECORD LOCKED—[d]:[filespec]
> This indicates a probable disk, disk drive, or other hardware problem. Refer to Appendix D. (PIP)

ERROR: FILE NOT AVAILABLE—[d]:[filespec]
> The file you are trying to access has been opened by another program. It must be closed before you can access it. (CHSET)

ERROR: FILE NOT FOUND—[d]:[filespec]
> Try using the r option if you are trying to copy a system file. Otherwise, check your spelling and syntax and which directory or user number you are in. (PIP)

ERROR: FILE NOT FOUND INVALID DISK SELECT—[d]:[filespec]
> You specified an unacceptable drive designation. Those accepted are A-H, M, N, O, and P. (PIP)

ERROR: FILE NOT FOUND NONRECOVERABLE—[d]:[filespec]
> This indicates a probable disk, disk drive, or other hardware problem. Refer to Appendix D. (PIP)

ERROR: FIRST SET d:[protect = on]
> You have tried to set a password before enabling password protection. (SET)

ERROR: HEX RECORD CHECKSUM—[d]:[filespec]
> This indicates a truncated or corrupted hexadecimal file. Use a backup file or recreate the damaged one. (PIP)

ERROR: ILLEGAL COMMAND TAIL
ERROR: ILLEGAL OPTION OR MODIFIER
ERROR: INVALID COMMAND OPTION
> You have used an unacceptable option with this command. Review the command description for the correct ones. (SDIR)

ERROR: INVALID DESTINATION—[d]:[filespec]

You have entered an unacceptable destination designation. Check for wildcards (not allowed) or proper devices used. (PIP)

ERROR: INVALID FORMAT
You have used incorrect syntax in your command statement. (PIP)

ERROR: INVALID FORMAT WITH SPARSE FILE—[d]:[filespec]
You tried to reformat or concatenate a sparse file. (PIP)

ERROR: INVALID HEX DIGIT—[d]:[filespec]
This indicates a truncated or corrupted hexadecimal file. Use a backup file or recreate the damaged one. (PIP)

ERROR: INVALID SEPARATOR
You must use only a comma to separate filenames in your command statement. (PIP)

ERROR: INVALID SOURCE
You have entered an unacceptable source designation. Check for wildcards (not allowed) or proper devices used. (PIP)

ERROR: INVALID USER NUMBER
Acceptable user numbers are from 0 to 15 only. (PIP)

ERROR: MAKE FILE—[d]:[filespec]
This indicates a probable disk, disk drive, or other hardware problem. Refer to Appendix D. (PIP)

ERROR: MAKE FILE ALREADY EXISTS—[d]:[filespec]
This indicates a probable disk, disk drive, or other hardware problem. Refer to Appendix D. (PIP)

ERROR: MAKE FILE INVALID DISK SELECT—[d]:[filespec]
You specified an unacceptable drive designation. Those accepted are A-H, M, N, O, and P. (PIP)

ERROR: MAKE FILE INVALID FILENAME—[d]:[filespec]
File names must be only eight characters and must not contain unacceptable characters. (PIP)

ERROR: MAKE FILE LIMIT EXCEEDED—[d]:[filespec]
You may not proceed until some of the files now open are closed. (PIP)

ERROR: MAKE FILE NONRECOVERABLE—[d]:[filespec]
This indicates a probable disk, disk drive, or other hardware problem. Refer to Appendix D.

ERROR: MAKE FILE R/O DISK—[d]:[filespec]
This indicates a probable disk, disk drive, or other hardware problem. Refer to Appendix D. (PIP)

ERROR: NO DIRECTORY SPACE—[d]:[filespec]
Use another disk or erase files to make room in the directory for a new file. (PIP)

ERROR: NO HELP.HLP FILE ON CURRENT DRIVE
You must load the file HELP.HLP on your current drive in order to have access to it. (HELP)

ERROR: OPEN FILE—[d]:[filespec]
This indicates a probable disk, disk drive, or other hardware problem. Refer to Appendix D. (PIP)

ERROR: OPEN FILE INCOMPATIBLE MODE—[d]:[filespec]
Some other process has opened this file. It must be closed before you can access it. (PIP)

ERROR: OPEN FILE INVALID DISK SELECT—[d]:[filespec]
You specified an unacceptable drive designation. Those accepted are A-H, M, N, O, and P. (PIP)

ERROR: OPEN FILE INVALID FILENAME—[d]:[filespec]
This indicates a probable disk, disk drive, or other hardware problem. Refer to Appendix D.

ERROR: OPEN FILE INVALID PASSWORD—[d]:[filespec]
You must enter the correct password in order to copy this file. (PIP)

ERROR: OPEN FILE LIMIT EXCEEDED—[d]:[filespec]
The file you are trying to access has been opened by another program. It must be closed before you can access it. (PIP)

ERROR: OPEN FILE NONRECOVERABLE—[d]:[filespec]
This indicates a probable disk, disk drive, or other hardware problem. Refer to Appendix D.

ERROR: PARAMETER REQUIRED, try SET [HELP]
Check the syntax in your command line entry. You must specify a parameter. (SET)

ERROR: PRINTER BUSY
This printer is being used by another process. You must wait for it to finish or terminate that process before accessing the printer. (PIP)

ERROR: QUIT NOT FOUND
You did not specify a quit string parameter. Enter PIP alone and use the * prompt when using strings. (PIP)

ERROR: RECORD TOO LONG
Hexadecimal records must not exceed 80 characters when using the H or I option. (PIP)

ERROR: SOME OTHER PROCESS HAS AN OPEN FILE
    You cannot have any open files when using this utility. (INITDIR)

ERROR: START NOT FOUND
    Your start string parameter could not be found in the source file.
    Check the file for the correct string. Enter PIP alone and use the *
    prompt when using strings. (PIP)

ERROR: TOO MANY ENTRIES IN INDEX TABLE
    NOT ENOUGH MEMORY
    There are too many programs running to be able to load this one also.
    Stop another program to make room. (HELP)

ERROR: UNABLE TO CLOSE HELP.DAT
    UNABLE TO CLOSE HELP.HLP
    The disk directory is full. Erase files to make room for more or use
    another disk. (HELP)

ERROR: UNABLE TO MAKE HELP.DAT
    UNABLE TO MAKE HELP.HLP
    Either the disk is full or the files are set to read only. Erase files to
    make room for more or use another disk or reset the files to read/write
    with the SET command. (HELP)

ERROR: UNEXPECTED END OF HEX FILE—[d]:[filespec]
    The hexadecimal file that you are trying to copy has been truncated.
    Use a backup copy or recreate the file. (PIP)

ERROR: USER ABORTED
    The operation has been canceled from the keyboard. If it was unin-
    tentional, the command must be reentered, it cannot be resumed.
    (PIP)

ERROR: VALID PRINTER NUMBERS ARE FROM 0 TO 4
    You entered a printer number that was unacceptable. Reenter the com-
    mand PRINTMGR START with the correct printer number.
    (PRINTMGR)

ERROR: VERIFY—[d]:[filespec]
    PIP could not verify the data written to disk. This indicates a prob-
    able disk, disk drive, or other hardware problem. Refer to Appendix
    D.

ERROR: WRITING FILE, CHECK DISK
    The destination disk is full or is write protected. Erase files to make
    room for more, use another disk, or remove the write protect tab
    from the disk. (WINDOW)

ERROR: WRITING FILE HELP.DAT
ERROR: WRITING FILE HELP.HLP

> The destination disk is full. Erase files to make room for more or use another disk. (HELP)

ERROR: WRONG PASSWORD

> You have attempted to reset a disk drive or file that is protected. Enter the correct password to continue. (SET)

ERROR: YOU HAVE NOT ENABLED ANY PRINTERS FOR PRINT MANAGER OUTPUT
AT LEAST ONE PRINTER MUST BE SPECIFIED

> You must reenter PRINTMGR START n and specify n as a printer number from 0 to 4.

ERROR: YOUR SYSTEM DOES NOT SUPPORT THAT PRINTER NUMBER

> The printer number that you entered does not exist in your system. Reenter an acceptable number. (PRINTMGR)

Fatal control (CONTROL.BR) error
[Specific Error]

> If you receive this message, your process has been interrupted and you have been sent back to the operating system. Before resuming the process, the error must be corrected. The specific errors are listed below. See the "BACKREST.DOC" file on the reference disk (5 of 5) for more information. (BACK/REST)

> Specific Errors
>> Badly formed filename
>> Control file not found
>> Delete flag should be T or F
>> Drive differs from previous PATH:
>> Duplicate record
>> Function should be C, N, or A
>> Illegal disk drive specified
>> Incomplete control file
>> Invalid number specified
>> Invalid record
>> Missing colon
>> Parameters should be T or f

Fatal error !! [specific message]

> If you receive this message, your process has been interrupted because of an I/O error in hardware (disk or computer) and you have been sent back to the operating system. Before resuming the process, the error must be corrected. The specific errors are listed below. See the

"BACKREST.DOC" file on the reference disk (5 of 5) for more information. (BACK/REST)

Specific Message

Can't append to DIR.BR
Can't open REPORT.BR or DIR.BR. Backup aborted.
Can't open RESTRPT.BR or DIR.BR. Backup aborted.
Can't open or close DIR.BR. Backup aborted.
Can't open or close RESTORE.BR. Restore aborted.
Can't read DIR.BR.
Can't read RESTORE.BR.
Handling PATHS.BR file. Backup aborted.
Sector error on control file [filespec]
Undetermined write error on report file.
Undetermined write error on work file.
Write error on work file. Backup aborted.

Control drive matches destination for drive [d:], Aborted backup.
Improper destination drive select for drive [d:], Aborted backup.
There is a defective control record in your CONTROL.BR file. (BACK/REST)

Must be Concurrent 3.2. Backup aborted.
You are using a different version of Concurrent than the one shipped with this utility. (BACK/REST)

No more directory space for report file.
No more directory space for work file.
No more disk space for report file.
No more disk space for work file.
There is no more space either in the directory or on the disk itself for more data. Delete files to make space or use another disk. (BACK/REST)

Not enough memory to run.
See "'Out of memory" in Appendix D. (BACK/REST)

File allocation table is defective.
The partition of your hard disk that you are trying to access is defective. Try again. If you get the same message, you will have to delete all files and reformat the partition. (HDMAINT)

File creation error
There is no more space on the destination disk. Delete files to make space or use another disk. (COPY)

File: [d]:[filespec] not found.
Concurrent cannot find the menu file specified. Check your spelling or the directory that you are accessing. (EDITMENU)

File in use.
>A process in another window currently has that file open. You must close the file before you can copy it. (COPY)

File is read/only.
>You must SET the file to read/write before you can change the command header. (CHSET)

File not found.
>Concurrent cannot find the menu file specified. Check your spelling or the directory that you are accessing. (CHSET, DIR, ERASE, ERAQ, TYPE)

Filename requested is not an acceptable file name.
>You have not named your file correctly. Review the conventions for naming files. (WINDOW)

Formsize and Pagesize must not differ by more than 100.
>Alter the values you have entered to conform to the rules for this utility. (PRINTMGR)

Formsize must be at least two lines greater than Pagesize.
>Alter the values you have entered to conform to the rules for this utility. (PRINTMGR)

HDMAINT cannot create a partition beginning at cylinder [nnn] because of a bad block in the reserved operating system area.
>You are trying to create a partition in a defective area of the hard disk. Relocate the partition or have the disk serviced. (HDMAINT)

HDMAINT cannot write a loader because no space is reserved for a system in this partition.
>The partition was not established to be bootable. Use FORMAT to make a new bootable partition after deleting all files from that partition. (HDMAINT)

HDMAINT cannot write a loader because a user file named DIRBIO.COM or DRIDOS.COM already exists.
>You must delete these existing files before Concurrent can write new system loader files on that partition. (HDMAINT)

HELP.DAT not on current drive.
>This file must be on the drive on which you create a HELP.HLP file. (HELP)

Initialization failed, no memory. EDITMENU abort.
>See the "Out of Memory" section of Appendix D. (COPYMENU, EDITMENU)

Insert system diskette in A: then press Ctrl/Alt/Del
> The hard disk system loader has failed. You must now load Concurrent from diskette.

Insufficient disk space
> There is no more space on the destination disk. Delete files to make space or use another disk. (COPY)

Invalid additional memory allocation, ignored.
> You entered an unacceptable value. See Chapter 11 for rules on setting values. (ADDMEM)

Invalid attribute
> You are trying to set an inappropriate attribute for a file. Review the options available under SET. (SET)

Invalid command
> The command you have entered is inappropriate in this context. Use the Alt-X command to cancel. (DR EDIX)

Invalid command option
> The option you have specified is inappropriate for that context. See Chapter 11 for the correct options. (CHSET, DIR, ERASE, ERAQ)

Invalid date
Enter new date: _____
> You must use the format mm-dd-yy to enter dates. Reenter at the prompt. (DATE)

Invalid drive
Invalid drive specification
> You specified a disk drive that does not exist in your system. Valid drives are A–H, M, N, O, and P.

Invalid 8087 state, ignored.
> You can only specify ON or OFF for this command. You entered something else. (8087)

Invalid entry number
> You entered a number that was not in the menu prompt. (STOP)

Invalid filename: [filespec]
Invalid filespec.
Invalid filespec (drive:filename:extension:password)
> Some part of your file specification is incorrect. Check your spelling or review syntax. (CHSET, COPY, DIR, REName, TYPE)

Invalid hard disk partition
> The hard disk system loader has failed. You must now load Con-

current from diskette. Copy all files from that partition before re-formatting it.

Invalid memory allocation size, ignored
> You entered an unacceptable value. See Chapter 11 for rules on setting values. (COMSIZE)

Invalid ORDER filetype, ignored.
Search order = CMD, COM, EXE, BAT
> You used an incorrect filetype extension. (ORDER)

Invalid parameter
> You specified an inappropriate parameter for an option you have selected. (SET)

Invalid partition table
> Either Concurrent cannot boot from the hard disk or there is a failure of the hard disk. You must use your diskette to restart Concurrent. Copy all files from the affected partition and recreate the partition, making sure that it is bootable.

Invalid path
> You specified an incorrect directory sequence. Check typing and syntax. (CHDIR, MKDIR, RMDIR, SYSDISK)

Invalid printer number, ignored.
> You specified a printer by a number that doesn't exist. You must reenter a correct number. (PRINTER)

Invalid response
> You must respond with a Y or N to this prompt for yes or no. (DR EDIX)

Invalid suspend state, ignored.
> You must enter ON or OFF only as settings for this command. (SUSPEND)

Invalid syntax. Correct syntax is as follows:
B>CHSET FILENAME [field = setting, field = setting, field = setting]
> Check your spelling or syntax and enter again. (CHSET)

Invalid time. Enter new time: _____
> You must use the format hh:mm:ss for entering the time. (TIME)

Invalid user number
Invalid user number, ignored.
> You have specified a user number outside the range 0–15. (COPY, USER)

Invalid wildcard.
> You can only use wildcards in this utility if they are in the same place in both old and new names. (REName)

Memory size set by COMSIZE is insufficient to load program.
> You did not set a memory allocation large enough. Use COMSIZE again to increase the memory to that needed by the program you are trying to run. (COMSIZE)

Menu corrupted
> The menu you have created is too large to fit on the screen. You must adjust it with EDITMENU. (RUNMENU)

Menu directory corrupted
> The MENU.DAT or your specified menu file contains entries that cannot be read. Use EDITMENU to recreate the file. (RUNMENU)

Missing directory
> You have left out a directory or subdirectory from its sequence. (CHDIR, MKDIR, RMDIR, SYSDISK)

Missing operating system
> There is no operating system on the hard disk partition that you have accessed. Start Concurrent from diskette and use HDMAINT to create a bootable partition.

No buffer has that file.
> You have specified a file that cannot be found in a buffer. Enter Alt-P to see which files are in which buffers. (DR EDIX)

No communication option installed
> You have specified a serial port that does not exist. Use the menu version of SETPORT to see which ports exist. (SETPORT)

No CP/M (DOS) label currently exists, and there is no room in the directory to make a new one.
> Delete files from the partition to make room in the directory. (HDMAINT)

No CPM.SYS or CCPM.SYS file on the hard disk.
> You have not copied Concurrent to this hard disk partition. Start the system from diskette and use PIP or COPY to transfer these files to the hard disk.

No file
> Concurrent cannot find the file that you have specified. Check spelling, syntax, and the user number or directory. (DIR, ERASE, REName, FUNCTION)

No help file
>The file HELP.EDX cannot be found. It must be on drive A: or the current drive to be accessed. (DR EDIX)

No operation was taken
>You must load PRINTMGR first and then enable your printers. (PRINTMGR)

No pattern
>You are trying to search but have not specified a pattern. (DR EDIX)

No source block
>You must first mark a block to be moved with Alt-K before you attempt to do anything with it. (DR EDIX)

No space for directory
>The disk directory space is full. You must erase a directory to be able to create a new one. (MKDIR)

No space reserved for a system on [d:]
>You must use HDMAINT or FORMAT to create a bootable partition for PC DOS on this partition. (REDOS)

No such file to rename.
>The file specified does not exist. Check spelling or command syntax. (REName)

No system files found, try another disk.
Mount a DOS system disk in A: then press any key.
>The disk you tried to boot from does not contain the operating system. (REDOS)

No system or bad system on boot disk!
>The PC DOS partition of your hard disk has a defective or missing operating system file. You must use HDMAINT to create a new bootable partition.

Not a valid CHSET field.
The valid fields are 8087, SHARED, and SUSPEND.
>You entered an unacceptable option to this command. Reenter with an acceptable option. (CHSET)

Not a valid CHSET setting.
>You entered an unacceptable setting for an option with this command. Review the command parameters in Chapter 11 and reenter. (CHSET)

Not allowed to change NUMBER field.
>You entered an additional number under WINDOW CHANGE. Use

the TOP, not the CHANGE subcommand under the WINDOW command to change windows. (WINDOW)

Not a valid WINDOW subcommand.
Check your spelling or syntax. You can enter CHANGE, FULL, TOP, VIEW, WRITE, or the first letter only under this command. (WINDOW)

Not enough memory for DOS file: CCPM.SYS

Not enough memory to load system. (CP/M)
You have installed the operating system on your hard disk, but your system does not have enough memory for it to be loaded into RAM.

Not enough room for a system on [d:]
The destination disk is too full to accept the operating system. Erase files to make room for more or use another disk. (REDOS)

Not erased: [filespec] currently opened.
Some process is using the file that you are attempting to erase. You must wait until it is through or close the file before you can erase it. (ERASE, ERAQ)

Not erased: [filespec] read only.
You attempted to erase a file that is set to read only. Use SET to make it read/write. (ERASE, ERAQ)

Not found.
You entered a pattern that could not be matched in the file. (DR EDIX)

Not renamed: [filespec] already exists, delete (Y/N)?
You attempted to use an existing file name to rename another file. If you respond Yes, the existing file is erased and the new file takes its name; if No, the operation is canceled. (REName)

Not renamed: [filespec] currently opened.
You cannot rename a file while it is open. Locate the process that has it in use, and close the file or wait until it becomes free. (REName)

Not renamed: invalid file.
Check your spelling or syntax and enter the command again. (REName)

No wildcards allowed.
You may not use wildcards in this command.

No WINDOW subcommand given.
You neglected to specify a subcommand under this command. (WINDOW)

Number required.
>   You must specify a line number when you use the Alt-G command. (DR EDIX)

One of the options is unknown or is not used correctly.
>   Check spelling or syntax and reenter the command. (PRINTMGR)

Open files on drives [d:. . .]
>   You are trying to terminate a process that has file(s) open on the drive(s) shown. They should be closed before terminating the process. (BDOS)

Out of range
>   You specified a line number with the Alt-G command that exceed the number in the file. (DR EDIX)

Overflow interrupt from [process] at address [nnnn.nnnn]
Press any key to stop process.
>   A multiply or divide operation has generated an overflow in the process named at the address shown. (XIOS)

Parity error from [process] at address [nnnn.nnnn]
Machine is halted!
>   An operation has generated a parity interrupt. The system must be turned off and on again. If it reoccurs, you may have a hardware problem. (XIOS)

Password error
>   You entered no password or the wrong one. Reenter the command with the correct one. (ERASE, ERAQ, REName)

Physical disk error
>   The disk you are trying to access is defective. (CHDIR, MKDIR, RMDIR, SYSDISK)

Printer busy.
Printer is being used by another program.
>   You have attempted to use a printer already in use by another process. Wait until it finishes or use STOP to terminate the other process. (CARDFILE, XIOS)

Printer [n] is not on line.
>   See that this printer is correctly cabled, turned on, and in an on-line condition. (XIOS)

Printer [n] is out of paper.
>   The printer shown has sent an out-of-paper signal to the operating system. Put in more paper. (XIOS)

Read error.
> Check spelling or syntax of the filespec entered. (DR EDIX)

Reading file HELP.HLP.
Reading HELP.HLP index.
> This indicates a probable disk, disk drive, or other hardware problem. Refer to Appendix D.

Read only disk.
> You must use SET to make this disk read/write or take the tab off the notch or cut a notch in the disk if none exists. (FUNCTION, MKDIR, RMDIR)

Requires Concurrent
Requires Concurrent Version 3.2
> You are trying to run a program or utility that requires the version of Concurrent it was written for.

Requires DOS media
> The drive you are accessing contains CP/M media. You can only use subdirectories on DOS media. (CHDIR, MKDIR, RMDIR, SYSDISK)

Reserved system area is defective.
> You must recreate the partition in another area of the hard disk. If the problem persists, your system has a hardware failure.

Response too long.
> You entered an unacceptable response, check spelling, or enter Alt-H to check appropriate responses. (DR EDIX)

Select error
> You specified an unacceptable drive designation. Those accepted are A-H, M, N, O, and P. Sometimes this also indicates a probable disk, disk drive, or other hardware problem. If it reoccurs, refer to Appendix D.

SETUP can't be run from a serial terminal.
> You may not use the SETUP command from any keyboard but the main system because it relies on the specific function keys. (SETUP)

Severe error—Restart the system.
> *Warning!* Restart only the print system with PRINTMGR START. If you perform a system reset (Ctrl-Alt-Del), you will not be able to resume printing but will have to start over. (PRINTMGR)

Source and destination diskettes are not of the same type.
> You must format the destination disk to match the source disk before you can copy under DSKMAINT. (DSKMAINT)

Source block is marked in some other buffer.
> You must remove the block marks in the other buffer before you can use them again. (DR EDIX)

Source menu file contains no menus.
> You must have a menu in the menu file for COPYMENU to be able to copy it. (COPYMENU)

Subcommand requires NUMBER = <0 – 3>
> You must specify an acceptable window number in a WINDOW command. (WINDOW)

System file is defective: CCPM. SYS (or CPM.SYS)
> Your CP/M or DOS hard disk partition is defective. Restart Concurrent from diskette and recreate that partition with HDMAINT after deleting all files. If the problem persists, your hard disk may need repair.

Text capacity exceeded.
> You have run out of memory for this program. All buffers should be written to disk and restart the program. (DR EDIX)

That job number does not refer to an active job.
> You have entered an inactive job number. Use the STATUS subcommand to determine the correct job number. (PRINTMGR)

That printer could not be enabled for output.
> Make sure that this printer is properly cabled, configured, turned on, and on-line. (PRINTMGR)

The acceptable values for [field] are [values]
> You entered an incorrect value for the specified field in the WINDOW command. Consult the value range offered in the message and enter a new one. (WINDOW)

The CP/M label has been password protected.
> You are trying to change a directory label that has been protected. Use SET to change the label so that HDMAINT can access it. (HDMAINT)

The destination is already a PC DOS system disk.
If you need to update it, use the PC DOS SYS command.
> The disk you have specified already contains the system files. (REDOS)

The disk you inserted contains backed-up files.
Please remove it and insert a new CP/M (DOS) media disk.
Touch return key when ready = = = >
> You should use blank disks for backup purposes in general; however,

if you wish to reuse old backup disks, you must enable them for reuse in your CONTROL.BR file. (BACK/rest)

The file specified in the command line cannot be opened.
>   This indicates a probable disk, disk drive, or other hardware problem. Try using a backup copy of the file. Refer to Appendix D.

The file specified in the command line was not found.
The menu file: [filespec] not found.
>   Check spelling, syntax, or other directories for the file you are trying to locate. (FUNCTION, COPYMENU)

The menu file [filespec] is corrupted.
>   The directory of the menu file is defective, possibly because the disk is defective. (COPYMENU, EDITMENU)

The printer requested is not set up for Print Manager output.
>   Use PRINTMGR TERMINATE to clear settings, then PRINTMGR START n (where n is printer number) to enable that printer. (PRINTMGR)

The Print Manager system job limit was exceeded.
>   You must wait to add any more jobs to the print queue. System capacity has been exceeded. (PRINTMGR)

The source and destination diskettes are different.
Do you want to format the destination diskette (Y/N)?
>   DSKMAINT requires that the source and destination disks be of the same format. (DSKMAINT)

The range of acceptable values for [field] is [values].
>   You entered an incorrect value for the specified field in the WINDOW command. Consult the value range offered in the message and enter a new one. (WINDOW)

The selected program could not be stopped.
>   You have tried to stop a program that is not running. (STOP)

The system drive is off.
>   You can't assign a system drive unless you have enabled that feature with the SYSDISK ON command. (SYSDISK)

This command/option requires CP/M media.
>   Certain Concurrent commands work with CP/M media only. (INITDIR, SET)

This [command] requires Concurrent 3.2.
>   The command specified can run only under the version of Concurrent with which it was shipped. (DSKMAINT, FUNCTION, SETPORT)

This program cannot be run from the serial terminal.
> You cannot run programs that require function key input from the serial terminal. (DSKMAINT, FUNCTION, SETPORT)

Too many bad blocks were found.
> The hard disk may be defective. Try to run the command again; if the problem persists, the hard disk will need to be serviced. (HDMAINT)

Too many directory entries for query.
> By using a wildcard, you have specified more files than the command can process. Break the group down into more manageable batches. (ERAQ)

Too many jobs were trying to access the Print Manager, try again.
> This is usually a temporary overload condition. Try again. (PRINTMGR)

Unable to continue: Type D for details.
> A hardware error has been detected. By entering D you will get a specific message. The list of such messages was given earlier in this section under "Disk Error Message Variations."

Unable to load file as generated.
> The hard disk does not yet contain the operating system. You must use PIP to copy the files to the desired partition.

Unable to make sense out of the options. See HELP.
> Check your spelling, syntax, or the option list for this command to correct the problem. (PRINTMGR)

Unable to open.
> This indicates a probable disk, disk drive, or other hardware problem. Refer to Appendix D. (FUNCTION)

Unable to rename system files.
> Try HDMAINT to verify that the system area is not defective, then try the REDOS command again. If the problem persists, recreate the partition. (REDOS)

Unable to write.
> This indicates a probable disk, disk drive, or other hardware problem. Refer to Appendix D.

Unexpected interrupt.
> The program generating the interrupt cannot run under Concurrent. You must also restart Concurrent to resume processing.

Unexpected system error. Can't continue.
>The utility has encountered an unanticipated problem. Restart Concurrent and reenter the command. (COPYMENU, EDITMENU)

Unknown command. Press Alt-H for help.
>You have entered a command that the program does not recognize. (DR EDIX)

Use CMD or blank filetype in CHSET command line.
With blank filetype, CHSET assumes a filetype of CMD.
>Only CMD-type files can be affected by this command. (CHSET)

User floating drives are restricted to N: & O:
>Only these two drive designations are available for assignment to a "floating drive." (CHDIR)

Value is too small.
>The minimum memory allocation for a process is 64K. You tried to set a value below that. (SETUP)

Verification error.
>This indicates a probable disk or other hardware problem. Refer to Appendix D.

Warning: System error. Please check your hardware.
>This indicates a probable disk, disk drive, or other hardware problem. Refer to Appendix D.

Wildcards not allowed when using CHSET to change a setting.
>You may use wildcards to display but not to change settings under this utility. (CHSET)

Window manager already installed.
>You have tried to install the window manager on top of itself. (WMENU)

WINDOW requires a Concurrent system that supports windows.
WMENU requires a Concurrent system that supports window management.
Wrong version of CCPM.SYS
>These commands can run only under the version of the operating system with which they were supplied. (WINDOW, WMENU, SETUP)

WINDOW WRITE command requires FILE =
WINDOW WRITE command requires TYPE =
>You must specify both a file name and a filetype with this subcommand. (WINDOW)

Write error (other than device full).
>This indicates a probable disk, disk drive, or other hardware problem. Refer to Appendix D.

Wrong volume . . . Please insert in drive [d:] disk volume [nn]
Touch return key when ready.
>You inserted the wrong disk. Use the disk with the volume number prompted for in the message. (back/REST)

You must supply a job number with DELETE (0 to 253).
>You must specify which job to delete. Use the STATUS subcommand to decide the proper job number. (PRINTMGR)

You used a key word incorrectly. See HELP.
>Check spelling, syntax, or the format option list in order to enter a correct format command. (PRINTMGR)

APPENDIX D

BASIC TROUBLESHOOTING
TECHNIQUES

When things go wrong, it's frustrating. Many times we are so involved in a problem that the answer to our dilemma is staring us in the face but we just can't see it. So the first rule of troubleshooting is to relax. Take a deep breath. Rub your eyes. Stare at the ceiling for a minute.

Now, look at the machine. Did you leave a disk drive door open? Are you trying to write a file to a protected disk? Did you add enough memory for that program to run? Run through the suggestions listed here before you panic. Consult a friend. Sleep on it. Only if the problem persists should you need to contact your software or hardware dealer. Imagine how embarrassed you will feel if the solution is something obvious.

When you do contact a dealer or manufacturer, have your facts in order. Have the serial numbers of the software and your hardware on hand. Be able to describe your system configuration, amount of RAM, number of drives, peripherals, and so on. Be able to describe in detail what you were doing when the system failed: what programs were running, what system messages appeared on the screen, and so on.

Digital Research maintains a hotline to provide you with assistance on your problem. Call (408) 646-6464 to talk to a technical support engineer, who can help you if the problem involves the Concurrent PC DOS operating system. There is also help available on DR SIG on the CompuServe Consumer Information Service. Just enter Go PCS-13 and leave a message in Section 4 or read the files in Data Library 4.

Also, make sure that you are not mixing different versions of operating systems or trying to run commands from a different version. Most Concurrent commands are designed to run only under the operating system version with which they are shipped.

POWER ON?

Chances are you will know whether there is power to the computer, but how about to a peripheral device? Are you sure that they are all turned on? You could have a loose power cable or interface cable to a satellite disk drive, modem, mouse, or other device. Does the printer or plotter have a trip switch indicating an out-of-paper condition, ribbon malfunction, or other deficiency? Power can be interrupted by bad board connections, faulty switches, bad power strips, and so on. Check each carefully, isolating each element before testing. However, if you are not experienced with electronic equipment, don't open up any machines. Leave it to the experts. Besides, you may void a warranty.

DRIVES AND FILES

Both disk drives and files can be set to Read Only. That is, you can look at what's there and copy from it, but you cannot "write" on it or make any changes to what's there. Use the SET command to enable files to be written upon. If you switch disks when a file is still open, you will not be able to write on the new disk. This is to protect you from possibly damaging data on the new disk because you still thought you were writing to the old disk. In addition, floppy disks can be physically protected from being overwritten by covering the "write enabling" notch on the side with an adhesive tape.

Are you having trouble finding something? You are probably looking on the wrong drive. Concurrent looks for a file only in the current or user number and user 0 in CP/M media and in the current directory on DOS media. Unless you specify another drive or directory, Concurrent will not look there. Also, make sure that you are specifying valid drive or directory names. Concurrent accepts drive designations A through H, the RAM or Memory disk (M), and the "floating drives" N and O and the system drive P. Review the information on drive and directory search paths.

Are you using passwords? If you have a drive that is labeled and has password protection enabled, you will need a password to access any protected files on that drive. By using the SDIR command, you can see which files are protected. By using the SET command you can enable password protection. Be sure that you keep a list of your passwords somewhere. If you forget them, you will not be able to access those files.

Do you know about the Sys and Dir attributes? Files with the Dir attribute can be accessed only in the current user number or current directory. Files with the Sys attribute can be accessed in other user numbers and drives. For example, program files set to Sys in User 0 or the root directory can be accessed from any directory or user number on that drive. To see which programs have been set to Sys, use the commands SDIR or DIR/S.

DISK HYGIENE

Did you put the disk in correctly? The open oval slot side should be the first into the machine, and the disk label should be under your thumb. If you close the drive door without a disk in the drive, you will get an on-screen system message. If the disk is upside down, the same thing will occur.

Make sure that you know where your disks are. On the other hand, if the disk drive door is open, even with a disk inserted, it cannot be read, because Concurrent doesn't know its there. Be sure you know which drive is which. With hard disk partitions, satellite floppy drives, and so on, you may lose track of which drive you are trying to access.

Have you switched disks without closing the file(s) on the one removed? If you do this, you will not be able to write to the new disk.

Could the disk be damaged? If you get an error message while Concurrent is accessing a floppy disk, your disk may be defective. If you suspect that it is, you should copy as many files as possible to a good disk and reformat the old disk with DSKMAINT. It may be salvageable. Those files that cannot be copied are probably lost.

If the jacket is damaged but the disk inside is intact, you can perform "surgery" and transplant your salvaged disk into a new jacket. Cut open the old jacket and carefully remove the disk from the damaged jacket. Slit the label end of a fresh jacket open with a razor blade, remove the disk, and insert the salvaged disk into the new jacket. Tape up the slit carefully. Don't get it upside down! If the disk has a stretched or warped center hole, you may be able to add additional reinforcing rings to the center hole and then be able to read the disk.

There are "disk doctor" utility programs that allow you to salvage damaged data or files that have been erased accidentally. If this is a recurrent problem, you may want to invest in such a set of utilities.

Are you trying to read a double-sided disk on a single-sided drive? The reverse can be done, but single-sided drives can only use single-sided disks (i.e., where data are recorded on each side separately). These disks can accommodate such data on both sides, however, if they have a notch on each side. You have to turn the disk over, however, to read the other side. Remember, when either of these notches is covered, that side cannot have data written to it.

Has anything happened that could "corrupt" a file on your disk? A power surge or "spike" could have damaged data in a file. Defective programs can damage files. If you suspect any of these types of problems, back up what you can and proceed cautiously with expendable data until you have isolated the problem.

Hard disk problems? You must use HDMAINT to format your hard disk for CP/M media or DOS media or create a partition for each if both are to coexist on the hard disk. (Each is given a different drive designation, i.e., C, D.) If you receive an error message while Concurrent is accessing the hard disk, it might indicate that a defective area has been detected. You should back up that partition and reformat it with HDMAINT. Documentation for HDMAINT is found on Disk 5 of the Concurrent End User Diskette set, not in the User's Guide.

OUT OF MEMORY?

Programs of the type COM and EXE often need more memory than Concurrent allots them and this needs to be adjusted. Review the ADDMEM and COMSIZE commands in Chapter 11. Those programs that require more memory than Concurrent has allotted them simply won't run unless you allocate more memory to them.

If you find that you are pushing the RAM limits of your system, there are several things you can do to alleviate the immediate situation. The first thing to do is run the STOP command on an unused window. That will tell you how much memory each of your programs or commands is using. You can terminate any of these from the window that you are in.

Some programs, when they load, take all remaining memory for themselves. You should identify these programs and remember to load them last so that they don't prevent you from running something else. If you have the WINDOW command running, you can recapture additional memory by using WMENU to remove it. You can tell if it is installed by the telltale "Win" on the status line.

By methodically checking your system and analyzing your work habits, most problems can be overcome.

APPENDIX E

CONCURRENT, VERSION 5, ENHANCEMENTS

The most recent version of Concurrent is called V 5.0 and includes several new features. Only a few of them affect the user directly. They are:

Command line recall and editing

I/O redirection

Added options to the SETUP main menu

The ability to use memory above 640K

First let's talk about command line recall and what it means. If you mis-type a command, you must reenter the entire command in order to correct the mistake. If the command line was long, then retyping it becomes a chore. If only the designers of the operating system had allowed you to bring back the last line, you could edit it, rather than re-enter it! PC DOS does in fact allow you to recall the last line (F3 key), as does CP/M Plus (an 8 bit DRI operating system). However PC DOS does not provide you with a really good set of editing commands as does Concurrent V5.0. Concurrent allows you to recall the line, move to the first character in the line, move to the last character in the line, move forwards or backwards, and insert or replace characters. Concurrent V 5.0 provides a 512 byte command line buffer, which means that you will be able to recall more than one prior command line. The number of command lines available for recall depends on the size of each of the commands, up to a total of 512 characters (minus some system markers). Continued use of this feature results in a feeling of "how did I ever manage without this?"

The next new feature is I/O redirection. Long a feature of UNIX,™ I/O redirection comes in very handy when you want to send information that would normally appear on your screen to a file on disk instead. For instance, suppose you wanted to get a listing of the files in a particular directory on disk, and then edit it for printing. Without I/O redirection this would be difficult. However in V 5.0 all you have to do is the following:

A>dir>dirlist.dat

Concurrent will execute the directory command and instead of displaying the results on the screen, Concurrent will re-direct the output to a file called "dirlist.dat." You can then edit the file with your favorite text editor. Similarly, you can redirect input (we redirected output in the last example). In this case, you might have a file that contains all the input that a program needs to execute. In this way we can change an application from a program that might only use the keyboard and screen to one that uses disk files, without having to change a line of code in the application. See the V5.0 Users Guide for complete details.

The changes to SETUP reflect some internal changes made to Concurrent that made it easier for you to change some physical devices.

The final improvement allows for the use of the expanded memory solutions that have become available in the PC marketplace recently. Because of the design of the IBM PC, the maximum amount of memory available to a user has been limited to 640K. At the time the PC was introduced 640K seemed like quite a lot. However, that is no longer the case. Many popular applications have grown in size as well as the size of the data from users. Notably Lotus™ users have created very large spreadsheets that cannot fit inside the 640K boundary. Therefore some new hardware solutions (new memory boards) have become available to go around the 640K limitation. Concurrent has been modified so that it can take advantage of some of these boards.

INDEX